POWER TO PRAY ONCE

AND RECEIVE

ANSWERS

LEAVING YOUR PRAYER ROOM
FILLED WITH ANSWERED PRAYERS

PRAYER M. MADUEKE

PRAYER
PUBLICATIONS
UNITED STATES

ISBN: 979-8685474049

Published by Prayer Publications

259 Wainwright Street, Newark,

New Jersey 07112 United States.

From The Author

Prayer M. Madueke

CHRISTIAN AUTHOR

My name is Prayer Madueke. I'm a spiritual warrior in the lord's vineyard. An accomplished author, speaker and expert on spiritual warfare and deliverance. I've published well over 100 books on every area of successful Christian living. I'm an acclaimed family and relationship counselor with several of titles dealing with those critical areas in the lives of the children of God. I travel to several countries each year speaking and conducting deliverance, breaking the yokes of demonic oppression and setting captives free.

I will be delighted to partner with you also in organized crusades, ceremonies, marriages and marriage seminars, special events, church ministration and fellowship for the advancement of God's kingdom here on earth.

All my books can be found <u>Amazon.com</u>. Visit my website <u>www.madueke.com</u> for powerful devotionals and materials.

Free Book Gift

Just to say Thank You for getting my book: Power to Pray once and Receive Answers, I'll like to give you these books for free:

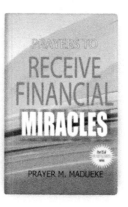

The link to download them are at the end of this book.

Your testimonies will abound. <u>Click here</u> to see my other books. They have produced many testimonies and I want your testimony to be one too.

Prayer Requests Or Counselling

Send me an email on <u>prayermadu@yahoo.com</u> if you need prayers or counsel or you have questions. Better still if you want to be friends with me.

Table Of Contents

CHAPTER ONE

THE ANCIENT LAND MARK

Every doctrine of the scripture is meant to be practical in the life of every believer who is expected by God to live to His glory:

> *"But as he which hath called you is holy, so be ye holy in all manner of conversation; because it is written, Be ye holy; for I am holy." 1Peters.1:15, 16.*

Believers are called by God to live a holy life in all manner of conversation. Holiness of life is a provision from God to every believer to receive. Every thing that Jesus suffered to provide for us should not be taken lightly. This precious doctrine is an experience expected from every believer and must not be taken lightly for any reason.

All believers are called unto holiness and every one of us as Christians are expected to respond immediately.

> *"For God hath not called us unto uncleanness, but unto holiness."* 1Thessalonians . 4:7

Holiness is the nature of God and was originally imparted into man who is the crown of God's creation. It is a divine establishment in the heart of man in the day of creation when He said: *"let us make man in our own image".* Man lost this image but Christ went to the cross of Calvary and paid the price to restore this wonderful experience to us as believers. Any Christian who is serious does not speak or think lightly of all that Christ did on the cross of Calvary. Believers by faith are called to receive this experience without merit or work but by faith. Holiness is an ancient land mark and should not be tampered with by any preacher no matter his position in the body of Christ. The Lord warned the children of Israel not to tamper with their neighbours land mark. If God warned against removing your neighbours land mark, how much more God's own land mark

"Thou shalt not remove thy neighbour's landmark, which they of old time have set in thine inheritance, which thou shalt inherit in the land that the Lord thy God giveth thee to possess it." Deuteronomy 19:14.

No matter the effect of the western development around us, God's standard for believers should not be modified or modernized by any one. The changing situation of the world around us should not be allowed to affect the doctrine of God:

"Remove not the ancient landmark, which thy fathers have set." Proverbs. 22:28.

God who is the ancient of days and Jesus Christ our saviour never change and the doctrine of God are still the same and can never change. Infact, God Himself placed a curse upon anyone who removes his neighbour's land mark and all the people around at that time echoed amen to His decree.

"Cursed be he that removeth his neighbour's landmark. And all the people shall say, Amen." Deuteronomy. 27:17.

Tampering with God's doctrine attracts a curse right from the beginning. Our God is still the same yesterday, today and forever, both in mercy, judgment, love, wisdom, power and knowledge. He has not changed an inch. No body is allowed to substitute sham for reality. God cannot accept our second best when it comes to the doctrine of holiness and the totality of His word:

"And Solomon made all the vessels that pertained unto the house of the Lord: the altar of gold, and

the table of gold, whereupon the shewbread was,
And the candlesticks of pure gold, five on the right
side, and five on the left, before the oracle, with
the flowers, and the lamps, and the tongs of gold,
And the bowls, and the snuffers, and the basins,
and the spoons, and the censers of pure gold; and
the hinges of gold, both for the doors of the inner
house, the most holy place, and for the doors of
the house, to wit, of the temple." 1Kings 7:48-50.

Many preachers today are modernizing the standard of God. The lifestyle of so many Christians and their leaders are disgracing to God's word. Their ways are contradictory to God's ways. Many modern preachers are enemies of the doctrine of holiness

"Why, seeing times are not hidden from the
Almighty, do they that know him not see his days?
Some remove the landmarks; they violently take
away flocks, and feed thereof." Job 24:1,2,

Modernist of our generation Christians are violently removing the ancient land mark. The famine of the true preaching of God's word on holiness is visible in many pulpits. The few who preach about it fail to live a holy life. Very few believers are still contending for the faith.

"Beloved, when I gave all diligence to write unto you of the common salvation, it was needful for me to write unto you, and exhort you that ye should earnestly contend for the faith which was once delivered unto the saints." Jude 1:3

THE UNCHANGING WORD OF GOD

The Lord warned the children of Israel that they should not add unto His word or diminish anything from it. Nobody has the right to argue the written word of God otherwise the person will incure the wrath of God.

> *"Ye shall not add unto the word which I command you, neither shall ye diminish ought from it, that ye may keep the commandments of the Lord your God which I command you."*
> *Deuteronomy 4:2*

Right from the time of the old, God has warned all not to tamper with His word to suit them in any generation. Doing that takes away the true light of God from a person or place.

> *"To the law and to the testimony: if they speak not according to this word, it is because there is no light in them." Isaiah. 8:20*

The book of Malachi says that God cannot change no matter the situation. Jesus is the same yesterday, today and forever. His word is everlasting, unchangeable at all times, places and situation.

> *"Being born again, not of corruptible seed, but of incorruptible, by the word of God, which liveth and abideth for ever. For all flesh is as grass, and all the glory of man as the flower of grass. The grass withereth, and the flower thereof falleth away: But the word of the Lord endureth for ever. And this is the word which by the gospel is preached unto you." 1Peter. 1:23-25*

No matter what is going on anywhere, in all the part of the world, the word of God remained the same. God's word abideth forever, endures forever and can never be corrupted.

"Verily I say unto you, this generation shall not pass, till all these things be fulfilled. Heaven and earth shall pass away, but my words shall not pass away." Mathew 24:34, 35

The word of God is perfect and needs no modification or development from anyone.

"The law of the Lord is perfect, converting the soul: the testimony of the Lord is sure, making wise the simple." Psalm 19:7

THE MEANING OF HOLINESS

Holiness simple means freedom from sin, to make sacred or holy. It is to be cleansed from moral corruption and pollution. Holiness is the absence of sin or to be free from the power of sin.

> *"I speak after the manner of men because of the infirmity of your flesh: for as ye have yielded your members servants to uncleanness and to iniquity unto iniquity; even so now yield your members servants to righteousness unto holiness. But now being made free from sin, and become servants to God, ye have your fruit unto holiness, and the end everlasting life." Romans 6:19, 22*

Holiness is God's demand from Him to His children, believers, people who are already born again. It is an experience after salvation. At salvation, the shoots of sin are destroyed but at holiness the roots of sin is destroyed giving ways for righteousness to flow from the heart.

> *"Knowing this, that our old man is crucified with him, that the body of sin might be destroyed, that henceforth we should not serve sin."* Romans 6:6

Holiness destroys desires for sin and gives a believer perfect hatred over every sin. At salvation, believers struggle to overcome certain sin but at holiness, he effortlessly lives above sin

> *"For we know that the law is spiritual: but I am carnal, sold under sin. For that which I do I allow not: for what I would, that do I not; but what I hate, that do I. I find then a law, that, when I would do good, evil is present with me. For I delight in the law of God after the inward man: But I see another law in my members, warring against the law of my mind, and bringing me into*

captivity to the law of sin which is in my members. O wretched man that I am! Who shall deliver me from the body of this death? I thank God through Jesus Christ our Lord. So then with the mind I myself serve the law of God; but with the flesh the law of sin." Romans 7:14-15, 21-25.

Sin cuts the joy of a believer at salvation but when a believer is holy, there is fullness of joy even in time of tribulation he still manifests full joy and perfect peace.

"And they stoned Stephen, calling upon God, and saying, Lord Jesus, receive my spirit. And he kneeled down, and cried with a loud voice, Lord, lay not this sin to their charge. And when he had said this, he fell asleep." Acts 7:59, 60

Every good student of the bible knows that the scriptures teach about two fold nature of sin. The sin outside and the sin living inside. When someone gets born again, actual sins committed are forgiven but with time the shoots of sin begin to show up again from the root. The believers at that point needed a purging and purification right from the inside. At conversion level, sin is not completely destroyed from inside. Believers do not love sin, he fights to overcome it. But the root keep on producing it, trying to overcome the believer. At that level, the joy of a believer is under attacks. His initial testimonies are questioned. His initial new professed life, love, peace with God are being questioned by forces of sin coming from the root inside. Shoots of sin begin to rear their heads trying to overcome the believer. He then begins to question his initial confessed freedom from sin: "Am I really born again?" At that point, the believer does not really commit sin but he knows that there is filthiness inside of him that needed to be cleansed

"Having therefore these promises, dearly beloved, let us cleanse ourselves from all filthiness of the flesh and spirit, perfecting holiness in the fear of God." 2Corinthians 7:1

He knows that there is a power inside trying to dominate, corrupt and destroy his initial testimony

"Behold, I was shapen in iniquity; and in sin did my mother conceive me." Psalm 51:5

Every Christian at conversion experience must pass through this stage. Living with this experience is very dangerous as it can bring backsliding. A constant unquenchable desire for a particular sin or sins in the life of a particular believer, is an evidence that such a believer is in need of a second touch from God to perfect the work of his salvation.

Trying to manage Christian life with such experiences is very dangerous. Many believers, at that point, may gradually go back into sin and constantly commit such sin from time to time. Some can begin to criticize others without really knowing the full consequences. Others can gradually begin go back into worldliness, lust, anger, evil passion, dressing like the world without seeing what is wrong.

The old nature will gradually come back and they began to sin in a Christian way. That is modern Christian lifestyles. They can be angry, commit fornication, indulge in gossips, worldly pleasures and enjoyment.

"Whoso is partner with a thief hateth his own soul: he heareth cursing, and bewrayeth it not."
Proverbs 29:24

Such so called believers are everywhere in many churches today. They are among the choristers, ushering, group, prayer warriors and among the ministers. Some commit fornication, adultery, habour unforgiving spirit and yet they profess to be Christians and even ministers. Some have gone into the level of having a reprobate mind with bible in their hands preaching in their mouth and their two feet in the pulpits.

"Because that, when they knew God, they glorified him not as God, neither were thankful; but

became vain in their imaginations, and their foolish heart was darkened. Professing themselves to be wise, they became fools. And even as they did not like to retain God in their knowledge, God gave them over to a reprobate mind, to do those things which are not convenient; Being filled with all unrighteousness, fornication, wickedness, covetousness, maliciousness; full of envy, murder, debate, deceit, malignity; whisperers, Backbiters, haters of God, despiteful, proud, boasters, inventors of evil things, disobedient to parents, Without understanding, covenant breakers, without natural affection, implacable, unmerciful:" Romans 1:21, 22, 28-31

CHAPTER TWO

JESUS CHRIST'S PRAYER FOR THE SANCTIFICATION OF HIS FOLLOWERS

Our savior, Jesus Christ, saw this threat in his disciples. They were with Christ, followed him every where but they still had the presence of the old man, the sin nature. These people were born again, they left their worldly profession, earthly ambition and answered the call of God

"And Jesus, walking by the sea of Galilee, saw two brethren, Simon called Peter, and Andrew his brother, casting a net into the sea: for they were fishers. And he saith unto them, Follow me, and I will make you fishers of men. And they straightway left their nets, and followed him. And

going on from thence, he saw other two brethren, James the son of Zebedee, and John his brother, in a ship with Zebedee their father, mending their nets; and he called them. And they immediately left the ship and their father, and followed him." Mathew 16:15-17, *"He saith unto them, But whom say ye that I am? And Simon Peter answered and said, Thou art the Christ, the Son of the living God. And Jesus answered and said unto him, Blessed art thou, Simon Barjona: for flesh and blood hath not revealed it unto thee, but my Father which is in heaven." Matthew 4:18-22*

They knew Christ, professed and preached him publicly. They forsook everything to follow Christ. They have faith in Christ, they have the right to go to heaven. They cast out demons. They had the power over evil spirit and devils were subject to them. They trod over serpents and scorpions and over every power of the enemy and nothing hurt them. Their names were written in the kingdom of heaven but their characters did not give them the fitness to enter heaven even though they had the right. (Matt. 19:27-29, Lk. 10:17-24)

They were born again but they were still struggling over position in the church. There are many leaders in the body of Christ with an enviable position but they still tell lies to be promoted. They want to be Assistance General Overseers, State Pastors, and Regional Overseers. They bribe their ways to take another man's position. They criticize others, run others down and tell horrible lies to be recognized by men and women in authority. They prefer the favour of men and position to God's recognition.

"And they departed thence, and passed through Galilee; and he would not that any man should know it. For he taught his disciples, and said unto them, The Son of man is delivered into the hands of men, and they shall kill him; and after that he is killed, he shall rise the third day. But they understood not that saying, and were afraid to ask him. And he came to Capernaum: and being in the house he asked them, what was it that ye

disputed among yourselves by the way? But they held their peace: for by the way they had disputed among themselves, who should be the greatest. And he sat down, and called the twelve, and saith unto them, If any man desire to be first, the same shall be last of all, and servant of all. And he took a child, and set him in the midst of them: and when he had taken him in his arms, he said unto them, whosoever shall receive one of such children in my name, receiveth me: and whosoever shall receive me, receiveth not me, but him that sent me." Mark 9:30-37

Today, the modernists are modernizing everything. In the olden days, the godfathers rebuke sin. The sons of the godfathers report their sins to the godfathers for prayers and restoration but today reverse is the case. That is the evidence of old man. Godfathers give position to their unqualified sons and daughters in the Lord. Their sins are forgiven them ever before they commit them. Murmuring and backbiting are increasing because of misplacement of position by those who have long legs, people at the top etc

"And Jesus going up to Jerusalem took the twelve disciples apart in the way, and said unto them, Behold, we go up to Jerusalem; and the Son of man shall be betrayed unto the chief priests and unto the scribes, and they shall condemn him to death, And shall deliver him to the Gentiles to mock, and to scourge, and to crucify him: and the third day he shall rise again. Then came to him the mother of Zebedee's children with her sons, worshipping him, and desiring a certain thing of him. And he said unto her, what wilt thou? She saith unto him, Grant that these my two sons may sit, the one on thy right hand, and the other on the left, in thy kingdom. But Jesus answered and said, ye know not what ye ask. Are ye able to drink of the cup that I shall drink of, and to be baptized with the baptism that I am baptized with? They say unto him, we are able. And he

saith unto them, ye shall drink indeed of my cup, and be baptized with the baptism that I am baptized with: but to sit on my right hand, and on my left, is not mine to give, but it shall be given to them for whom it is prepared of my Father. And when the ten heard it, they were moved with indignation against the two brethren. But Jesus called them unto him, and said, ye know that the princes of the Gentiles exercise dominion over them, and they that are great exercise authority upon them. But it shall not be so among you: but whosoever will be great among you, let him be your minister; And whosoever will be chief among you, let him be your servant: Even as the Son of man came not to be ministered unto, but to minister, and to give his life a ransom for many."
Matthew 20:17-28

When Jesus saw the condition of His disciples, He prayed for their sanctification or holiness

"Sanctify them through thy truth: thy word is truth. As thou hast sent me into the world, even so have I also sent them into the world. And for their sakes I sanctify myself, that they also might be sanctified through the truth. Neither pray I for these alone, but for them also which shall believe on me through their word; That they all may be one; as thou, Father, art in me, and I in thee, that they also may be one in us: that the world may believe that thou hast sent me." John 17:17-21.

After Abraham was ninety and nine years, God still demanded that he should be perfectly holy

"And when Abram was ninety years old and nine, the Lord appeared to Abram, and said unto him, I am the Almighty God; walk before me, and be thou perfect." Genesis 17:1.

So, the uniform teaching of both old and New Testament says that holiness is for those who are in the Lord already, who need to be perfect in the heart. Unbelievers need justification but believers need perfection.

"And now, Israel, what doth the Lord thy God require of thee, but to fear the Lord thy God, to walk in all his ways, and to love him, and to serve the Lord thy God with all thy heart and with all thy soul," Deuteronomy 10:12

"Be ye therefore perfect, even as your Father which is in heaven is perfect." Matthew 5:48

Without holiness of life, no believer is fit to enter into heaven even though he has the right. Two person born of the same parents may have the right to a blessing upstairs but if one is lame, even though he has the right, he may not be fit to climb up to take his blessings. Sin incapacitates believers and renders them unfit for heaven when they are not dealth with from the root

"Finally, brethren, farewell. Be perfect, be of good comfort, be of one mind, live in peace; and the God of love and peace shall be with you. But as he which hath called you is holy, so be ye holy in all manner of conversation; because it is written, be ye holy; for I am holy." 1Peter 1:15, 16, 2 Corinthians 13:11,

HOLINESS, THE GATE WAY INTO HEAVEN

Heaven is the eternal destiny of the saints of all ages, a place where the saints will be with Christ eternally. This holy city will accommodate the saints who will make it eventually. Jesus Christ spoke concerning this city in different ways. The apostles spoke about this city called heaven. Heaven is a material one not mystical

"Let not your heart be troubled: ye believe in God, believe also in me. In my Father's house are many mansions: if it were not so, I would have told you. I go to prepare a place for you. And if I go and prepare a place for you, I will come again, and receive you unto myself; that where I am, there ye may be also." John 14:1-3

Our Lord Jesus Christ called it His father's house and he promised to come back and take the saints into it where He will live with us, the saints forever

"When Christ, who is our life, shall appear, then shall ye also appear with him in glory." Col. 3:4

The uniform teaching of the scripture affirmed that this place is not a permanent place but a transit and a place where we shall get ready for a permanent place. The rapture is the time when Christ comes up to the air to catch up all true believers in Christ. Any believer who is not ready for the rapture now is in a terrible danger.

"Beloved, now are we the sons of God, and it doth not yet appear what we shall be: but we know that, when he shall appear, we shall be like him; for we shall see him as he is. Father, I will that they also, whom thou hast given me, be with me where I am; that they may behold my glory, which

thou hast given me: for thou lovedst me before the foundation of the world. And I heard a great voice out of heaven saying, Behold, the tabernacle of God is with men, and he will dwell with them, and they shall be his people, and God himself shall be with them, and be their God." 1John 3:2, John 17:24, Revelation 21:3. Heaven is real and a place to be prepared for. Jesus spoke about it, the saints saw it and wrote about, it "And I John saw the holy city, new Jerusalem, coming down from God out of heaven, prepared as a bride adorned for her husband." Revelation 21:2

"And there came unto me one of the seven angels which had the seven vials full of the seven last plagues, and talked with me, saying, Come hither, I will shew thee the bride, the Lamb's wife. And he carried me away in the spirit to a great and high mountain, and shewed me that great city, the holy Jerusalem, descending out of heaven from God, Having the glory of God: and her light was like unto a stone most precious, even like a jasper

stone, clear as crystal; And had a wall great and high, and had twelve gates, and at the gates twelve angels, and names written thereon, which are the names of the twelve tribes of the children of Israel: On the east three gates; on the north three gates; on the south three gates; and on the west three gates. And the wall of the city had twelve foundations, and in them the names of the twelve apostles of the Lamb. And he that talked with me had a golden reed to measure the city, and the gates thereof, and the wall thereof. And the city lieth foursquare, and the length is as large as the breadth: and he measured the city with the reed, twelve thousand furlongs. The length and the breadth and the height of it are equal. And he measured the wall thereof, an hundred and forty and four cubits, according to the measure of a man, that is, of the angel. And the building of the wall of it was of jasper: and the city was pure gold, like unto clear glass. And the foundations of the wall of the city were garnished with all manner of precious stones. The first foundation was jasper;

the second, sapphire; the third, a chalcedony; the fourth, an emerald; The fifth, sardonyx; the sixth, sardius; the seventh, chrysolite; the eighth, beryl; the ninth, a topaz; the tenth, a chrysoprasus; the eleventh, a jacinth; the twelfth, an amethyst. And the twelve gates were twelve pearls; every several gate was of one pearl: and the street of the city was pure gold, as it were transparent glass. And I saw no temple therein: for the Lord God Almighty and the Lamb are the temples of it. And the city had no need of the sun, neither of the moons, to shine in it: for the glory of God did lighten it, and the Lamb is the light thereof. And the nations of them which are saved shall walk in the light of it: and the kings of the earth do bring their glory and honour into it. And the gates of it shall not be shut at all by day: for there shall be no night there. And they shall bring the glory and honour of the nations into it." Revelation 21:3, 9-26.

John in his vision of the end was taken to a high mountain where he was shown this holy city which he described as great. According to John, this city has the fullness of God's glory in it, God's full light. It is called the "Bride" because of its virgin beauty, unstained with sin and the maker of this great holy city is God Himself. In this city, John saw the full blazing, brilliant glory of God. All that is there are transparent, clear as crystal, like unto a clear glass. It is a wonderful city with everything in it reflecting the glory of God visible in all points at all time without obstruction. For John to see fully like this, it means that the place is a ready made, waiting for the church to be ready to enter it.

"And he shewed me a pure river of water of life, clear as crystal, proceeding out of the throne of God and of the Lamb. In the midst of the street of it, and on either side of the river, was there the tree of life, which bare twelve manner of fruits, and yielded her fruit every month: and the leaves of the tree were for the healing of the nations. And there shall be no more curse: but the throne of

God and of the Lamb shall be in it; and his
servants shall serve him: And they shall see his
face; and his name shall be in their foreheads.
And there shall be no night there; and they need
no candle, neither light of the sun; for the Lord
God giveth them light: and they shall reign for
ever and ever." Revelation 22:1-5

Those, who by God's grace, find themselves into this great city, shall hunger no more, neither thirst any more. In the city, there is a river of the water of life as a constant reminder that our Lord Jesus Christ gives life in reality. In the midst of the great city is the tree of life yielding different types of fruits each month. Inside the city is everything we need and will ever need. The leaves of the tree are for the healing of the nations because no one who enters the city will ever get sick.

"But ye are come unto Mount Zion, and unto the
city of the living God, the heavenly Jerusalem,
and to an innumerable company of angels, To the
general assembly and church of the firstborn,

which are written in heaven, and to God the Judge of all, and to the spirits of just men made perfect, And to Jesus the mediator of the new covenant, and to the blood of sprinkling, that speaketh better things than that of Abel. For he looked for a city which hath foundations, whose builder and maker is God. And make straight paths for your feet, lest that which is lame be turned out of the way; but let it rather be healed. Follow peace with all men, and holiness, without which no man shall see the Lord: Looking diligently lest any man fail of the grace of God; lest any root of bitterness springing up trouble you, and thereby many be defiled; Lest there be any fornicator, or profane person, as Esau, who for one morsel of meat sold his birthright."
Hebrew 12:22-24, 11:16

The question is this, who are the people that will enter into this great city? It is only meant for true believers who are sanctified. They have the privilege with God to enter and remain with God forever and ever. Those who will enter heaven are believers, who despite the temptation and trials of their faith, live overcomer life at the time of rapture or the point of death. They are believers who live a prevailing life on earth to overcome evil, false prophets, the world, persecution, Satan, sin, and live a holy life.

"And he that sat upon the throne said, Behold, I make all things new. And he said unto me, Write: for these words are true and faithful. And he said unto me, it is done. I am Alpha and Omega, the beginning and the end. I will give unto him that is athirst of the fountain of the water of life freely. He that overcometh shall inherit all things; and I will be his God, and he shall be my son." Revelation 21:17 "And he measured the wall thereof, an hundred and forty and four cubits, according to the measure of a man, that is, of the angel." Revelation 21:5-7, 2:7, 11, 17, 26-28, 3:5, 12, 21

Holiness is still God's standard to get to heaven. No one gets to heaven by any other means except by living a holy, victorious and triumphant life. It is still and will ever be God's demand for entering heaven, no matter your status in the body of Christ. For the Christians religion, holy life is the correct yardstick to go to heaven. All other ways are fruitless effort and every human effort is as good as nothing and worse than useless. Christ like life of holiness, the biblical holiness is the only true way to heaven. God demands it and that is what he expects.

> *"Follow peace with all men, and holiness, without which no man shall see the Lord:" Hebrew 12:14*

CHAPTER THREE

EXCLUSION FROM THE CITY

To be excluded from this great city is the worst thing that can happen to someone in life. You may be in the earthly prison for life. Banned from entering into any other city but to be excluded out of the city of God is worst than the worst that had ever happened put together. But the fact is that majority will yet be excluded. It is a hard fact to know and yet it is a fearful reality.

Though it is God's will for everyone to get into this great city. Only those who meet the requirement will be permitted to come into it.

> *"But the fearful, and unbelieving, and the abominable, and murderers, and whoremongers, and sorcerers, and idolaters, and all liars, shall*

have their part in the lake which burneth with fire
and brimstone: which is the second death."
Revelation 21:8.

The fearful will not be allowed (John 9:18-22, Matthew 10:33-36). The unbelieving will also be excluded out of the city (Jn. 3:18-20, 36). Those who are not courageous enough will be excluded from the city. The abominable shall also be excluded out of the city (Leviticus 18:21-27, Proverbs 6:16-19).

Those who commit any manner of abomination will not be allowed to enter the gate of heaven; God will frown at them that day. Another set of people that will not be allowed into the great city are the murderers (1Jh.3:15), whore mongers, fornicators, adulterers, the sorceress, witches and wizards. No liar of any level or an idolater will be given the opportunity to enter into heaven for a moment.

"And there shall in no wise enter into it any thing
that defileth, neither whatsoever worketh

abomination, nor maketh a lie: but they which are written in the Lamb's book of life." Revelation 21:27.

"For I testify unto every man that heareth the words of the prophecy of this book, If any man shall add unto these things, God shall add unto him the plagues that are written in this book: And if any man shall take away from the words of the book of this prophecy, God shall take away his part out of the book of life, and out of the holy city, and from the things which are written in this book." Revelation 22:18-19.

The bible standard still holds and will ever hold that, without holiness no one can see the Lord. So the standard of God for heaven still stands. They are unchangeable, without compromise and the word of God still says.

"Blessed are the pure in heart: for they shall see God." "But as he which hath called you is holy, so

be ye holy in all manner of conversation; because it is written, Be ye holy; for I am holy." Matthew 5:8, 1 Peter 1:15-16

Preachers, believers and sinners who are removing the ancient Land mark are under curse from the Almighty God.

"Why, seeing times are not hidden from the Almighty, do they that know him not see his days? Some remove the landmarks; they violently take away flocks, and feed thereof." Deuteronomy 27:17.

"Cursed be he that removeth his neighbour's landmark. And all the people shall say, Amen." Deuteronomy 19:14. "Thou shalt not remove thy neighbour's landmark, which they of old time have set in thine inheritance, which thou shalt inherit in the land that the Lord thy God giveth thee to possess it." Job 24:1, 2. I want to remind us again that His verdict is still the same as it was

of old: the wicked shall be turned into hell and all

nations that forsake God, whether they are

Overseers, Americans, Africans, Europeans or the

Asians. The truth is that judgment is coming on

the unrepentant world, no matter the nation

involved "The sinners in Zion are afraid;

fearfulness hath surprised the hypocrites. Who

among us shall dwell with the devouring fire?

Who among us shall dwell with everlasting

burnings?" Isaiah 33:14

We are warned on time that if our right eye, hand or any thing will offend us, we should cast them off for the scripture says that it is more profitable to enter heaven without the above than to have them and enter hell fire.

Matthew 2:24-30 "..........."

Today is still the day of grace and mercy. Salvation is still possible now. This is the day to seek the Lord. His favour is still very much available. Seek for His favour while you still have the opportunity.

"Seek ye the Lord while he may be found, call ye upon him while he is near: Let the wicked forsake his way, and the unrighteous man his thoughts: and let him return unto the Lord, and he will have mercy upon him; and to our God, for he will abundantly pardon." Isaiah 55:6, 7

In the last day, many great church leaders who neglected this word will regret it.

"And the Pharisees came forth, and began to question with him, seeking of him a sign from heaven, tempting him. And he sighed deeply in his spirit, and saith, why doth this generation seek after a sign? Verily I say unto you, There shall no sign be given unto this generation." Matthew 8:11, 12.

HELL IS REAL

I read a book sometime ago titled 4 hours interviews in hell, written by Yemi Bankole. In the dream, he saw hell inmates suffering beyond explanations. In his story, the first person he saw was a lady who called his name from hell fire. According to him, he said that the face of the lady was marred and disfigured by the fires of hell and the skin blackened by flames and littered by sores. Later, he discovered that the name of the lady is Rita, his former hostel mate in Grammar school. To him, Rita was a good Christian and died a good Christian.

"Rita, why are you here", he asked? We organized concerts, carols and quiz competitions and you did not disappoint God. Rita answered:" yes I did all that in the grammar school. But, later in life and two months to my graduation in the university, I yielded to a sinful affair with a boy at home during a short break. I thought of repenting in the campus chapel when the school resumed. But returning from home, I had a motor accident. The next thing I discovered was that I found myself in the gate over there and the angel asked me to go to the left road which ends in this place." This may be your last chance to repent of your own sin, confess it and forsake it. You can pray for your sanctification and God will sanctity you.

The second person he saw in hell was a girl of about thirteen years old. He asked: "young girl why are you here?" The girl answered: "please give me water, water is my dire need now. I have been thirsty since 1932 when I came in here please, just a small quantity. "He asked again," "why are you here?" She answered and said:. "It was my mother. She initiated me into witchcraft at six. But before I reached twenty years and die, I killed seven hundred and twenty four people and became a registered witch in the spirit world. But a companion, who has been there since 1620 told me that the punishment there is eternal and the condition, is permanent. Is it true?" She asked.

Another person he saw was a late deaconess of his church, who died of arthritis. She was a woman of reputation in their church when she was alive. She was regarded as an incarnation of virtues and a paragon of philanthropy. "Mum, why did you come here, did you miss your way?" He asked

"Allen, this is what unforgiving spirit has for me as a record, she replied. It was discovered in the book of records that all my life was pleasant to God except the misunderstanding that happened between the choir master and me. By and large, I was older than he and as such I was expecting him to come and apologize, at least courtesy demands for that I was in this malice when death struck that same month" she explained. On the tombstone of the late woman is written the epitaph: Late madam Emily Adeyombo (Nee Beatrice) a loyal Christian soldier, who courageously fought for the holy course; carried her cross and kept the sword unsheathed. Your gentle spirit broke the bond of death when you were called home to rest in the bossom of God. Farewell and rest in perfect peace till the morning of resurrection. She was buried in the church yard in honour of her unalloyed Christian commitment. In the church-yard that Friday evening of her burial ceremony the minister in charge read 1Cor. Chapter 15:39-59 with resounding farewell words, "Good mother, good bye" till we meet again beside the river of life. People that day waved their hands to her remains and solemnly sang the first two stanzas of the heart-touching hymn of late J. Montgomery (1771-1854), for her interment.

But friends, instead of the rivers of life, she's in hunger, peril and untold pain.

He saw many people in hell, but let us talk about the next person last people who happened to be an acclaimed minister of God, this minister contributed much to the early missionary activities in Nigeria and in other African states. Before his death, he was the overseer of his church when the founder died in the early fifties. He asked him, sir, what happened. "Dear, I never dreamt of coming to a place like here. Presently in heaven, are good number of those who heard these good teachings from me. But two years before death struck, I took part of the church money meant for church building to conduct a wedding ceremony for my grand daughter. And this been unknown to anybody, I let it go. At the end of that year, I wrote the financial report revealing that the whole amount contributed was spent for the project. After a sermon one Sunday evening I took ill which ended in my death. Before I got to the main gate, I was basking in joy that I had made it at last, not until I was directed here, I doubted it, until the book of record was opened which carried all my good Christian services. But underneath all the rendered services it was written "not to be render because he took a holy thing." The angel in charge further disclosed that the church money which I took was contributed out of sweat by the church member and the faithfulness demand for a just and true account. He added that my report was not in conformity with the gospel standard of stewardship and that the act betrayed my office as a minister", he explained. "But sir did you plead for mercy?" I asked. "I did but the angel replied that forgiveness is possible only in the world, but reward or judgment is determined there at the gate" he answered.

"For the time is come that judgment must begin at the house of God: and if it first begin at us, what shall the end be of them that obey not the gospel of God? And if the righteous scarcely be saved, where shall the ungodly and the sinner appear?"
1Peter 4:17, 18

Many ministers may not make it at last. One offence is enough to take one to hell fire. Beloved, I am guilty myself. I have been a pastor for years now and I became so familiar with God and the work that I took many things for granted. I am sorry for that and I plead for forgiveness and power to forsake every sin. This is a public confession both to God, the church and my leaders.

For many years, as a pastor, because of my Christian background, I tried as much as possible not to involve myself in money matters. But off late, I began to listen to peoples complain. At times, I see myself instructing the people that count money to give so and so person money for transport, welfare and at times for myself before totaling the money. This is against church administrative principles. Initially I thought I was right because almost every other pastor I knew was doing that. I thought that once I do not use the money to enrich myself, buy cars and live a life of pleasure, there is no problem.

Off late, just few years ago, I started neglecting little little sins that I used to hate before with perfect hatred just because majority were doing them. But one day, I came to myself and I prayed again and by his grace the Lord had mercy upon me and restored me completely. Holiness is still God's perfect and the only standard to go to heaven. The Day of Judgment can come any time, earlier than you think. In the Day of Judgment, sinners whoever lived, shall be judged by God. They will stand before the most righteous judge to give account of their deeds. Every secret thing each person had done, small and great will be judged. Every evil deed done, every intent, every evil word spoken, or evil purpose entertained, goes on record in heaven against the doer. Those whose names are not written in the book of life shall be cast into the lake of fire.

"And I saw the dead, small and great, stand before God; and the books were opened: and another book was opened, which is the book of life: and the dead were judged out of those things which were written in the books, according to their works." Revelation 20:12

All the drunkards, cheats, polygamous, etc. will appear before the judgment seat of Christ. John said that he saw the dead, small and great stand before God. The orphans were there, spinsters and bachelors were there too. The poor and the rich, tall and short, educated and illiterate etc all appeared before the great judgment day.

You may have been sanctified and made holy before, but now check your life. You may have little foxes, unprofitable conversation, the return of anger, unkind criticism, evil talks, murmuring against leadership, pride of God's gifts, revengeful spirit, partial obedience, worldliness, love of money, unholy competition, lying, pretence, financial mismanagement, evil liberty, worldly dressing, luxurious living or evil modernization, discouragement etc.

Today is a day of salvation, God can still save you, sanctify you and empower you again to be profitable to His kingdom more than ever before. For those who will not mind, who will ignore the warnings in this book, they will be forever banished outside the holy city and separated forever from God to the lake of fire. It is impossible, perfectly impossible to allow sin to profane the holy city.

"For without are dogs, and sorcerers, and whoremongers, and murderers, and idolaters,

*and whosoever loveth and maketh a lie."
Revelation 22:15,*

*"And there shall in no wise enter into it any thing
that defileth, either whatsoever worketh
abomination, or maketh a lie: but they which are
written in the Lamb's book of life." Revelation
21:27,*

*"And whosoever was not found written in the
book of life was cast into the lake of fire."
Revelation.20:15.*

Here again is the last and final invitation to who ever will, all who needed peace and perfect deliverance.

*"And the Spirit and the bride say, Come. And let
him that heareth say, Come. And let him that is
athirst come. And whosoever will, let him take the
water of life freely." Revelation 22:17*

CHAPTER FOUR

HOLINESS, GOD'S DEMAND FROM BELIEVERS

Sanctification, which is holiness, is an operation of the Spirit of God on those who are already in Jesus by which they are rendered increasingly holy. Holiness is not for the unbelievers. Sinners are called out of sin but believers are called unto holiness.

> *"Now the Lord had said unto Abram, Get thee out of thy country, and from thy kindred, and from thy father's house, unto a land that I will shew thee:" Genesis 12:1*

The first call of God to Abraham was a call out of sin and later in his life, God called him into holiness of life.

*"And when Abram was ninety years old and nine,
the Lord appeared to Abram, and said unto him,
I am the Almighty God; walk before me, and be
thou perfect." Genesis 17:1*

It is very essential to know and seek for what God demands from us as believers. God's permanent desire for every believer is to come to perfection. For anyone to enter into heaven, this is God's demand (1Pet. 14:15). This demand is for believers to really live life to the fullness of God's will. To be separated, and live righteously for God. Many believe that this demand is from God but that it is only for few people, like the ministers and other leaders in the body of Christ. As a result, many do not bother to attain to that level. However, this call is from God and He who wills our sanctification is also our sanctifier

*"For God hath not called us unto uncleanness, but
unto holiness. He therefore that despiseth,*

despiseth not man, but God, who hath also given unto us his Holy Spirit." 1 Thessalonians 4:7, 8

The call is not from a man, church or the government but from God. For this reason, it is not a doctrine to be accepted or rejected, if one likes. It is a must for every Christian.

IT IS A COMMANDMENT FROM GOD

"For I am the Lord your God: ye shall therefore sanctify yourselves, and ye shall be holy; for I am holy: neither shall ye defile yourselves with any manner of creeping thing that creepeth upon the earth. For I am the Lord that bringeth you up out of the land of Egypt, to be your God: ye shall therefore be holy, for I am holy." Leviticus 11:44, 45

These are God's children who came out from the (world) Egyptian lifestyle. He spoke to them through Moses but the words of command were not from Moses but from God who sent the words. God who created the creeping things does not want it to be used as an instrument of defilement to man. The creeping things were created for a purpose not for the purpose of man's defilement and pollution God wants man to be holy unto Him, that is, His demand from every believer who wishes to live with God eternally. For God to be proud enough to be identified as our God, any where, any time, we must be holy. The reason he saved us and gave us salvation is to bring us unto a level of holiness, so that he can proudly say these are my children that I called out from Egypt of sinful life. Everything that God created is for a purpose. He created money for a purpose. Every organ of our body is created for a purpose and the lack of understanding for God's purpose before using anything will bring defilement to man hence he warned the children of Israel against being defiled by unclean things.

"When the host goeth forth against thine enemies, then keep thee from every wicked thing. For the Lord thy God walketh in the midst of thy camp, to deliver thee, and to give up thine enemies before

thee; therefore shall thy camp be holy: that he see no unclean thing in thee, and turn away from thee." Deuteronomy 23:9, 14

Believers need to be holy at all times. In times of war, peace, when our enemies increase, we are expected to be holy. In times of sorrow, happiness and opposition, we still need to be holy. In our relationship, conversation with people, we still need to be holy. In times of opposition, distress, believers should avoid the carelessness that will defile them. In the midst of enemies, gossipers and oppression, we are still expected by God to be holy. God expects believers to keep their camp holy, undefiled, no matter how hot the battle may seem to be. The reason is because our God is everywhere present and he takes record of whatever a man does. Our camp, our lives should be clean and holy even in the midst of our enemies, problems or prosperity.

"For the Lord thy God walketh in the midst of thy camp, to deliver thee, and to give up thine enemies before thee; therefore shall thy camp be

holy: that he see no unclean thing in thee, and turn away from thee." Deuteronomy 23:14

When we enter any place as a believer, the Lord expects that as we come out, we should not be defiled. As we mix up with people, go to the school with them, and study under one teacher, we should not allow defilement to come unto our live. As we enter into any office, room, lecturer's office, court of law or police station, defilement should not be seen in our lives. At the end of any discussion with our boss, pastors, opposing groups, we are to present our bodies back to God holy.

"I beseech you therefore, brethren, by the mercies of God, that ye present your bodies a living sacrifice, holy, acceptable unto God, which is your reasonable service. And be not conformed to this world: but be ye transformed by the renewing of your mind, that ye may prove what is that good, and acceptable, and perfect, will of God." Roman 12:1, 2

Holiness is a demand from God to every believer. It is good to travel to any country if it is God's will but as we look out for permission, to get visa, we should come out of that office with pride that our bodies are not defiled. As we enter into any examination as believers, into any office to look for job, we should come out still as holy people. As we drive on the way, interact with friends in public and private places, we should at the end present our bodies as a living sacrifice, holy, still acceptable unto God. As we look at people, shake hands with opposite sex, plan for our wedding, discuss during courtship, at the end, the Lord expects that we present our bodies, all the parts of our organs, holy as a living sacrifice. As we approach our pastors, marriage committee to explain to them how we found out God's will in marriage, at the end, we are expected by God to present our bodies as a living sacrifice, holy accepted unto God. Before we go into prayers anywhere, before we leave our house every morning at all times, we must have settled every quarrel of any kind so as to present our bodies as a living sacrifice, holy acceptable to God.

As a Christian leader who is working under an unbeliever or whoever you are working with, God's demand is that as you present your files, messages or carry out your assignments, you should at the end of each encounter present your whole body, including the sensitive area of your body, as a living sacrifice, holy acceptable unto God. As you travel for official duty with your boss if you must, you should come back with a holy body that will be acceptable to God. What is a living sacrifice that is a acceptable? What is a reasonable service? It is living a daily consistent Christian holy life, no matter the pressure around you. God demands holiness from every believer. We may need to go to the same school with others who are not called unto holiness. We may have our office and live in the same house with them but God demands holiness. We must not be conformed to the latest fashion. We must not dress like them. We must not do our wedding like the people of the world even though we work in the same office with them and live in the same house with them. The reason is because, we are believers and believers are called unto holiness. Other pastors, ministers may be stealing church money to buy big cars and live big, do not join them. Not all ministers are believers. But you, as a believer, you are called unto holiness. Other ministers may be committing immorality and yet performing miracles, but you have a different call. Do not conform to the world.

"I beseech you therefore, brethren, by the mercies of God, that ye present your bodies a living sacrifice, holy, acceptable unto God, which is your reasonable service. And be not conformed to this world: but be ye transformed by the renewing of your mind, that ye may prove what is that good, and acceptable, and perfect, will of God." Roman 12:1, 2

Don't stay in the permissive will of God. The perfect will of God for every believer is to present their bodies a living sacrifice, holy, acceptable unto God. This is your reasonable service. All believers are called to live a life of separation from the world so that we can prove what is good and acceptable, perfect will of God.

In our dressing, we must not dress to attract men but to attract God. Our affections and desires must be separated and distinct from that of the world.

CHAPTER FIVE

WHAT IS HOLINESS?

1. It is called sanctification

    "Sanctify them through thy truth: thy word is truth. As thou hast sent me into the world, even so have I also sent them into the world. And for their sakes I sanctify myself, that they also might be sanctified through the truth." John17:17-19.

Jesus saw the need of this experience in the life of his apostles and he prayed to God to sanctify them through his truth which is his word. In 11Thessalonians. 4:3 Paul spoke about this experience, holiness, and referred to it as sanctification and the will of God, an experience that will help believers to abstain from fornication. In the same 11Thessalonians. 5:23, Paul again spoke concerning it and prayed for the church that the very God of peace should sanctify them whole, spirit, soul and body so as to be preserved blameless unto the coming of our Lord Jesus Christ.

2. Holiness

The only service wholly acceptable to God is the service rendered in holiness and according to the perfect will of God. This should be done before God all the days of our life

"In holiness and righteousness before him, all the days of our life." Luke. 1:75

Believers are expected to put on the new man which was created by God in righteousness and true holiness.

"And that ye put on the new man, which after God is created in righteousness and true holiness." Eph. 4:24

The call of God to believers is not to backslide or go back to compete with the world but we are called unto holiness

> *"For God hath not called us unto uncleanness, but unto holiness." 1 Thess. 4:7*

The life of uncleanness is forbidden by God in the life of a believer. The life of holiness is meant to be part of every believer's life. It is not optional or for some level of Christians. It is a universal Christian call from God. Believers all over the world are expected to attain the level of holiness, living the life of making peace every where and never to be identified with trouble making and trouble makers.

> *"For they verily for a few days chastened us after their own pleasure; but he for our profit, that we might be partakers of his holiness. Follow peace*

with all men, and holiness, without which no man

shall see the Lord:" Hebrews 12:10, 14,

In conclusion, concerning the word holiness as a requirement from God, Peter in his writing to Christian of his days said,

"As obedient children, not fashioning yourselves

according to the former lusts in your ignorance:

But as he which hath called you is holy, so be ye

holy in all manner of conversation;" 1Peter. 1:14,

15

In this passage, believers are expected to be obedient in every thing concerning God. No believer is expected by God to be spoken to concerning being disobedient again. In our relationship with God and one another, we should not fashion ourselves again according to the worldly standard or indulge in any character or way of life that can provoke lust, which was our way of life when we were ignorant about holiness. This is because the person we are living to please is not unholy but a holy God.

Believers are called to aspire to be holy not as our pastors, leaders or any other person but as God. That should be the competition that should be seen among believers.

3. Purity of heart

Pure heart is another popular word for holiness, which is what God demands from believers. Holiness includes both inward and outward. It is an experience that affects both inside and outside. Some people argue that what they do outside does not matter. Others say that what is happening inside them does not matter. True holiness affects our inner man and controls the thoughts, desires and imaginations right inside of a person.

> *"Who shall ascend into the hill of the Lord? Or who shall stand in his holy place? He that hath clean hands, and a pure heart; who hath not lifted*

up his soul unto vanity, nor sworn deceitfully."
Psalm 24:3, 4.

Holiness goes inside of a believer and purifies the heart. Pilate washed his hands but his heart was not pure. The holiness that God demands affects the soul of a man and betters the inside. No matter how good one feels that God is or the good things one receives from God, one will know it better, benefit from His goodness better, when one has his heart cleansed by God.

"Truly God is good to Israel, even to such as are of a clean heart." Psalm. 73:1.

The blessings of the Lord can fully be enjoyed and God fully seen in manifestation when believers surrender to God for the sanctification of their heart. Heart purity enables a believer to see God in every aspect of his life clearly and takes him to heaven at last.

"Blessed are the pure in heart: for they shall see God." Matthew. 5:8

4. Circumcision of heart

Circumcision of the heart is another word for describing holiness. A circumcised heart is empowered to love God perfectly above other things, places and persons. Circumcised heart has perfect peace and calmness that can give a believer a quality life.

"And the Lord thy God will circumcise thine heart, and the heart of thy seed, to love the Lord thy God with all thine heart, and with all thy soul, that thou mayest live." Deuteronomy. 30:6

The circumcision of the heart frees the heart from sin. It is an operation of God made without a visible hand.

The circumcision of the heart frees the heart from sin and destroys the roots of sin. It is an operation of God made without a visible hand

"In whom also ye are circumcised with the circumcision made without hands, in putting off the body of the sins of the flesh by the circumcision of Christ:" Colosians. 2:11

The work of circumcision, which is holiness, is done inwardly inside of a person. It is a spiritual exercise which no man can do except God. No one can penetrate into the heart with any power to touch the adamic nature except God be with you. The work of holiness is done by God, when believers fully believe and pray earnestly for the experience.

"But he is a Jew, which is one inwardly; and circumcision is that of the heart, in the spirit, and not in the letter; whose praise is not of men, but of God." Romans. 2:29

5. Perfection

Perfection is another term used for holiness. At the age of ninety nine God still demanded some level of perfection in His dealings with Abraham.

"And when Abram was ninety years old and nine, the Lord appeared to Abram, and said unto him, I am the Almighty God; walk before me, and be thou perfect." Genesis. 17:1.

No matter how holy a believer is, he cannot attain to God's level of holiness, so there is always the need to aspire for perfect perfection in our holiness exercises.

"Be ye therefore perfect, even as your Father which is in heaven is perfect." Matthew. 5:48

Our goal in holiness exercise should be a continous exercise to get to the level of God's holiness. Relaxing may affect our already attained level and can cause some ignorant believers to pattern their holiness at man's level. Every true believer should be glad to see others growing in the Lord, perfecting holiness.

"For we are glad, when we are weak, and ye are strong: and these also we wish, even your perfection." 2 Corinthians. 13:9

Holiness is perfect love which casteth out fear and brings boldness into the life of a believer

"Herein is our love made perfect, that we may have boldness in the Day of Judgment: because as he is, so are we in this world. There is no fear in love; but perfect love casteth out fear: because fear hath torment. He that feareth is not made perfect in love." 1John. 4:17, 18

HOLINESS, DIVINE REQUIREMENT FOR GETTING INTO HEAVEN

If you have everything else but you don't have holiness, you are not going to get to heaven. You may have the gifts of God, you may be outspoken, eloquent, have money, good job, you may even know how to present the truth in the best way, but if you do not have holiness, you will not get to heaven. With your gift of God, everybody may be waiting for you before you get to any place. People may be happy because they are benefiting from your natural and spiritual gifts, but if you do not have holiness, hell fire is anxiously waiting for you.

You may be useful to many people, millions of souls worldwide, you may have powerful popularity but except you have holiness you are useless to yourself and you amount to nothing before your creator.

What is holiness? Holiness is the nature of God, the love of God, the very essence of Christian living and Christian conduct. The believer who has this divine nature implanted in his heart will be able to do things that are well pleasing in

God's sight. With this nature of God in the life of a believer, he is perfectly humble and can never start a quarrel. This is because by nature, he is a peace maker.

> *"Now no chastening for the present seemeth to be joyous, but grievous: nevertheless afterward it yieldeth the peaceable fruit of righteousness unto them which are exercised thereby."* Hebrews 12:14

Believer's with this nature of God well rooted in them are disciplined, considerate and cannot be tribalistic, no geographical limitation in carrying out the great commission. They have no racial restriction or class distinction in the assignment of the great commission

They do not see themselves better than others or make others feel inferior because to a sanctified person, every body is equal before God. The sanctified believer has the perfect love of God planted in his heart.

"Though I speak with the tongues of men and of angels, and have not charity, I am become as sounding brass, or a tinkling cymbal. And though I have the gift of prophecy, and understand all mysteries, and all knowledge; and though I have all faith, so that I could remove mountains, and have not charity, I am nothing. And though I bestow all my goods to feed the poor, and though I give my body to be burned, and have not charity, it profiteth me nothing. Charity suffereth long, and is kind; charity envieth not; charity vaunteth not itself, is not puffed up, Doth not behave itself unseemly, seeketh not her own, is not easily provoked, thinketh no evil; Rejoiceth not in iniquity, but rejoiceth in the truth; Beareth all things, believeth all things, hopeth all things, endureth all things. Charity never faileth: but whether there be prophecies, they shall fail; whether there be tongues, they shall cease; whether there be knowledge, it shall vanish away." 1Corinthians. 13:1-8

CHAPTER SIX

HOLINESS, THE INDISPENSABLE EXPERIENCE

Holiness is an experience that we do not have to avoid. Man is born with sin in and out.

"Behold, I was shapen in iniquity; and in sin did my mother conceive me." Psalm. 51:5.

The inside of a man is very unclean, dirty and what ever is dirty will need to be cleansed and unfortunately that is the condition of man from the fall of Adam.

"And said unto them, Hear me, ye Levites, sanctify now yourselves, and sanctify the house of

the Lord God of your fathers, and carry forth the

filthiness out of the holy place." 2 Chronicles. 29:5

By the time King Hezekiah began to reign the house of God was polluted and filled with a lot of filthiness. A lot of evil was done in the house of God. At that time, both the people and the temple of God needed to be cleansed, washed to be and made pure before they could have fellowship with God

"And they gathered their brethren, and sanctified themselves, and came, according to the commandment of the king, by the words of the Lord, to cleanse the house of the Lord. And the priests went into the inner part of the house of the Lord, to cleanse it, and brought out all the uncleanness that they found in the temple of the Lord into the court of the house of the Lord. And the Levites took it, to carry it out abroad into the brook Kidron. Now they began on the first day of the first month to sanctify, and on the eighth day of the month came they to the porch of the Lord:

so they sanctified the house of the Lord in eight days; and in the sixteenth day of the first month they made an end." 2 Chronicles. 29:15-17

Those who are saved and called by God need cleansing of God before they can render acceptable service to God or qualify to cleanse the temple

"Wherefore gird up the loins of your mind, be sober, and hope to the end for the grace that is to be brought unto you at the revelation of Jesus Christ;" 1Peter. 1:3, 15,

"Sanctify yourselves therefore, and be ye holy: for I am the Lord your God." Leviticus. 20:7.

Those who are begotten by God and called, are expected to be holy and live a holy life. Another name for holiness is circumcision.

"And the Lord thy God will circumcise thine heart, and the heart of thy seed, to love the Lord thy God with all thine heart, and with all thy soul, that thou mayest live." Deuteronomy. 30:6.

This experience is for the regenerated souls who are already saved. The first work of grace is salvation while the second work of grace is sanctification. At salvation, we have right to heaven but at sanctification we have fitness to heaven. The holiness experience is very important for every born again Christian.

After Abraham had walked with God for ninety years, God still appeared to him and demanded for this indispensable experience.

"And when Abram was ninety years old and nine, the Lord appeared to Abram, and said unto him, I am the Almighty God; walk before me, and be thou perfect." Genesis. 17:1

God demanded for circumcision for the second time from the children of Israel. Holiness, sanctification or circumcision is the second definite experience for every believer.

"At that time the Lord said unto Joshua, Make thee sharp knives, and circumcise again the children of Israel the second time. And Joshua made him sharp knives, and circumcised the children of Israel at the hill of the foreskins. And this is the cause why Joshua did circumcise: All the people that came out of Egypt, that were males, even all the men of war, died in the wilderness by the way, after they came out of Egypt. Now all the people that came out were circumcised: but all the people that were born in the wilderness by the way as they came forth out of Egypt, them they had not circumcised." Joshua. 5:2-5.

Jonah was a child of God, called by God into the office of a prophet but he still had hatred for a whole nation called Nineveh

"And God saw their works that they turned from their evil way; and God repented of the evil, that he had said that he would do unto them; and he did it not." Jonah 3:10.

"But it displeased Jonah exceedingly, and he was very angry. And he prayed unto the Lord, and said, I pray thee, O Lord, was not this my saying, when I was yet in my country? Therefore I fled before unto Tarshish: for I knew that thou art a gracious God, and merciful, slow to anger, and of great kindness, and repentest thee of the evil. Therefore now, O Lord, take, I beseech thee, my life from me; for it is better for me to die than to live. Then said the Lord, Doest thou well to be angry?" Jonah 4:1-4.

"Then said the Lord, Thou hast had pity on the gourd, for the which thou hast not neither madest

it grow; which came up in a night, and perished in a night: And should not I spare Nineveh, that great city, wherein are more than sixscore thousand persons that cannot discern between their right hand and their left hand; and also much cattle?" Jonah 4:10-11

He had the gift of prophecy but he had no love for souls. The condition of Jonah called for holiness inside of him. If you have not overcome the work of the flesh, and the desires thereof, as a believer, you need sanctification. I am not talking of sinful life. You say that you are born again and you are living in sin, your salvation is not real. You need to re-visit Calvary for your salvation before you can talk of holiness. A believer does not live a sinful life. Believers are free from sin.

"Now the works of the flesh are manifest, which are these; Adultery, fornication, uncleanness, lasciviousness, Idolatry, witchcraft, hatred, variance, emulations, wrath, strife, seditions,

heresies, Envyings, murders, drunkenness, revellings, and such like: of the which I tell you before, as I have also told you in time past, that they which do such things shall not inherit the kingdom of God." Galatians. 5:19-21

"Notwithstanding in this rejoice not, that the spirits are subject unto you; but rather rejoice, because your names are written in heaven." Luke.10:20.

"And he said unto them, Go ye into all the world, and preach the gospel to every creature. He that believeth and is baptized shall be saved; but he that believeth not shall be damned. And these signs shall follow them that believe; in my name shall they cast out devils; they shall speak with new tongues;" Mark. 16:15-17

These are the disciples of Jesus Christ. They once lived above sin, they answered the call of God and all become ministers of God under the pastorship of Jesus Christ. They cast out demons, preached the gospel. The evil spirits were subjected to them and their names were written in the book of life. They knew the Lord but they did not have the holiness experience.

"Then came to him the mother of Zebedee's children with her sons, worshipping him, and desiring a certain thing of him. And he said unto her, what wilt thou? She saith unto him, Grant that these my two sons may sit, the one on thy right hand, and the other on the left, in thy kingdom. But Jesus answered and said, ye know not what ye ask. Are ye able to drink of the cup that I shall drink of, and to be baptized with the baptism that I am baptized with? They say unto him, we are able." Matthew.20:20-22

They were still struggling over position.

"And when the ten heard it, they were moved with indignation against the two brethren." Matthew. 20:24.

They were still having indignation against one another. Their hearts were still not right to each other, they were quarreling, fighting and planning evil right inside of their heart. Right in the front of Jesus, all these things were going on inside of His disciples. There was something inside them that was revolting against God, righteousness and their unity. Outside of them, it seemed that everything was all right, but there was a great problem living inside. They were impatient, critical and judgmental. Some of them wanted fire to come down from heaven to burn physical human beings like Elijah did. I need to clarify that when we call fire or pray die, we refer to spirits or power behind problems not human being.

However this means that when the unrepentant occult witch or wizard decide to wrap him or herself to the spirit, they may die and their blood will be upon their head. Believers in their prayers should target the main power behind problems, actions and not human being.

"And it came to pass, when the time was come that he should be received up, he steadfastly set his face to go to Jerusalem, and sent messengers before his face: and they went, and entered into a village of the Samaritans, to make ready for him. And they did not receive him, because his face was as though he would go to Jerusalem. And when his disciples James and John saw this, they said, Lord, wilt thou that we command fire to come down from heaven, and consume them, even as Elias did? But he turned, and rebuked them, and said, ye know not what manner of spirit ye are of. For the Son of man is not come to destroy men's lives, but to save them. And they went to another village." Luke 9:51-56

The disciples of Jesus Christ were judgmental and could not stand at the time of trouble. At the time Jesus Christ needed them most when he was suffering, they all forsook him and ran away. For believers to be able to live aright with, or around sinners in this world and maintain their Christian life, they must be holy, sanctified and circumcised in the heart, hence Jesus prayed for the sanctification of the true believers.

> "Sanctify them through thy truth: thy word is truth. As thou hast sent me into the world, even so have I also sent them into the world. And for their sakes I sanctify myself, that they also might be sanctified through the truth. Neither pray I for these alone, but for them also which shall believe on me through their word; That they all may be one; as thou, Father, art in me, and I in thee, that they also may be one in us: that the world may believe that thou hast sent me." John 17:17-21

Believers who will live for God on this earth need purification of the heart in order to obey the truth as demanded by God. We need to love people and one another with a pure heart and unfeigned love.

"Seeing ye have purified your souls in obeying the truth through the Spirit unto unfeigned love of the brethren, see that ye love one another with a pure heart fervently:" 1 Peter. 1:22

To be holy is to our advantage even on this earth before we get to heaven. With holiness, we can be guided to escape many troubles. Holiness can bring deliverance from death and direct our ways. When we talk about deliverance, holiness of life is a great agent for believers deliverance which can last and be preserved. A holy person who believes in deliverance can enjoy his Christian life to the full. But when someone who is not holy believes and practices deliverance, he may get delivered but he will not keep it for long. Such a person will end up doing deliverance all the time without being completely and perfectly delivered.

"The integrity of the upright shall guide them: but the perverseness of transgressors shall destroy them. Riches profit not in the day of wrath: but righteousness delivereth from death. The

righteousness of the perfect shall direct his way:
but the wicked shall fall by his own wickedness.
The righteousness of the upright shall deliver
them: but transgressors shall be taken in their
own naughtiness." Proverbs 11:3-6

Deliverance comes from God who lives in heaven above. Many deliverances that people are doing today is polluted and defiled because both the deliverer and the delivered are limited to the earth planet. True deliverance comes from God above. Some so called deliverance ministers do not know what holiness is all about. Those who have heard about holiness do not believe it. The few that believe it do not have the experience. Those who are being delivered are ignorant of the experience we are talking about. That is the reason why many deliverances are not permanent.

"Who shall ascend into the hill of the Lord? Or
who shall stand in his holy place? He that hath
clean hands, and a pure heart; who hath not lifted

up his soul unto vanity, nor sworn deceitfully."

Ps. 24:3, 4.

It is unfortunate that many people today ascend into the hills of the devil to get power but for the sanctified holy saints, they ascend into the hill of the Lord. No one can stand in the holy place and get true miracle, deliverance or any blessing from God that will last without having a clean hand, pure heart which is holiness. Those who wish to enjoy the dividend of their prayers and fasting for deliverance should think of holiness also in addition to other miracles they desire from the Lord. No one can lift up his soul to vanity and expect true and lasting deliverance from the Lord. It is a deceit to swear deceitfully, tell lies and still expect true and lasting deliverance from the Lord. No one can mock God, no matter how many times deliverance are done.

"Be not deceived; God is not mocked: for whatsoever a man soweth, that shall he also reap. For he that soweth to his flesh shall of the flesh reap corruption; but he that soweth to the Spirit

shall of the Spirit reap life everlasting." Galatians 6:7-8

As the day of the Lord is coming closer, believers are reminded to be sanctified and improved in the experience they have already by having all their conversation done in holiness, godliness, in peace without spot and blame.

"But the day of the Lord will come as a thief in the night; in the which the heavens shall pass away with a great noise, and the elements shall melt with fervent heat, the earth also and the works that are therein shall be burned up. Seeing then that all these things shall be dissolved, what manner of persons ought ye to be in all holy conversation and godliness, Looking for and hasting unto the coming of the day of God, wherein the heavens being on fire shall be dissolved, and the elements shall melt with fervent heat? Nevertheless we, according to his promise, look for new heavens and a new earth, wherein

dwelleth righteousness. Wherefore, beloved, seeing that ye look for such things, be diligent that ye may be found of him in peace, without spot, and blameless." 2 Peter 3:10-14

Those who really want to see Jesus and live with him eternally does not joke or play with this experience. Holiness is an indispensable experience that no child of God should ignore no matter the reason.

"Beloved, now are we the son of God and it doth not yet appear what we shall be: but we know that, when he shall appear, we shall be like him; for we shall see him as he is. And every man that hath this hope in him purifieth himself, even as he is pure." 1John 3:2, 3

Holiness is the perfect will of God for every true child of God. It is an indispensable experience that has no substitute.

"For this is the will of God, even your sanctification that ye should abstain from fornication:" 1Thessalonians 4:3.

"Wherefore Jesus also, that he might sanctify the people with his own blood, suffered without the gate. Let us go forth therefore unto him without the camp, bearing his reproach." Hebrew. 13:12, 13.

Jesus Christ died to pay the price of sanctification for believers. Any believer who fails to receive this wonderful experience is denying himself of a great benefit which Jesus suffered for.

"Elect according to the foreknowledge of God the Father, through sanctification of the Spirit, unto obedience and sprinkling of the blood of Jesus Christ: Grace unto you, and peace, be multiplied." 1Peter 1:2

When you consecrate yourself wholly to God and pray fervently, God will sanctify you.

CHAPTER SEVEN

PRIORITY OF HOLINESS

When we talk of holiness after salvation, we mean that it is superior in rank, position and of more privilege than other experiences be it power or any other. Every believer should give holiness a befitting attention above every other experience after salvation. Seeking any other thing above holiness after salvation could be dangerous. That is the real problem that the church of Jesus Christ is going through all over the world, today.

"Follow peace with all men, and holiness, without which no man shall see the Lord:" Hebrew. 12:14

Seeing God means a lot and also means many things. You may get power, anointing without holiness after your salvation but you may not see God even as you are manifesting His power. You can get a ministry and run it without being holy, you will not see God even in that ministry. A lot of things may be taking place around you but yet God will not be seen. You may have deliverance, business, breakthroughs without seeing God around you.

It is very dangerous to seek any other thing above holiness after your salvation. You can get deliverance and holiness together after your salvation but seeking for deliverance above holiness is very dangerous. It can ruin your Christian life and destroy all your efforts in life.

Holiness is what is going to determine your entrance into heaven.

"Who is like unto thee, O Lord, among the gods? Who is like thee, glorious in holiness, fearful in praises, doing wonders?" Exodus. 15:11

"For I am the Lord your God: ye shall therefore sanctify yourselves, and ye shall be holy; for I am holy: neither shall ye defile yourselves with any

manner of creeping thing that creepeth upon the earth. For I am the Lord that bringeth you up out of the land of Egypt, to be your God: ye shall therefore be holy, for I am holy." Leviticus. 11:44-45

"Give unto the Lord the glory due unto his name: bring an offering, and come before him: worship the Lord in the beauty of holiness." 1Chronicles. 16:29

Whatever we do with God, for God or in God without this holiness experience amount to nothing. Our prayers without holiness is nothing. Our service of any kind without holiness amounts to nothing. Our deliverance without holiness amounts to nothing. Our worship without holiness amounts to nothing. Our offerings, gifts without holiness amount to nothing. Every thing we do for God, in God and with God must be characterized with the beauty of holiness

"Who shall ascend into the hill of the Lord? Or who shall stand in his holy place? He that hath clean hands, and a pure heart; who hath not lifted up his soul unto vanity, nor sworn deceitfully."
Psalm. 24:3-4

A thorough study of the scriptures reveals that everything about God is associated with holiness. Unfortunately, believers pursue money, gifts blessings etc first before holiness. It has been discovered also that whatever we get after salvation without holiness always stands against our getting into the experience of holiness. And once you give power a chance to take the position of holiness, it is difficult to replace it again. Power wants to control every other thing around him. That is the misplacement in our modern Christian community worldwide. Once power takes the position of leadership after salvation, it does not want to allow holiness to take it's rightful position. Power can only surrender to holiness when holiness is first recognized before power and dully given its position before power comes in.

If you give wealth, pleasure etc the first position, they do not allow holiness to fully operate as expected by God. We are called as ministers unto holiness first, after salvation. Believers who receive ministry after salvation without the true experience of holiness will be one sided. Today, we see ministers and ministries who say that they are called to emphasize on prosperity, some say they are called to emphases on wealth, others said they are called to emphasis on evangelism but the problem is that these so called preachers may not have had the experience of holiness which is the second definite experience that comes by the grace of God. Ministers are called to preach the totality of God's word but when we come to the preaching of God's word, emphasis should be given to salvation first, holiness second, Holy Ghost baptism third etc. You can receive your ministry after salvation but your ministry should not be allowed to take the place of Holiness.

Even in the kingdom of darkness, there is hierarchy among them.

"For we wrestle not against flesh and blood, but against principalities, against powers, against the rulers of the darkness of this world, against spiritual wickedness in high places." Ephesians. 6:12

Power, wealth, prosperity and all manner of blessings, feel reluctant to give salvation its rightful place once they have been given the first or wrong position.

"Now when Jesus heard these things, he said unto him, Yet lackest thou one thing: sell all that thou hast, and distribute unto the poor, and thou shalt have treasure in heaven: and come, follow me. And when he heard this, he was very sorrowful: for he was very rich. And when Jesus saw that he was very sorrowful, he said, how hardly shall they that have riches enter into the kingdom of God! For it is easier for a camel to go through a needle's eye, than for a rich man to enter into the kingdom of God." Luke. 18:22-25

The greatest problem today in the body of Christ is the misplacement of priority and order of preference to basic Christian experiences. All over the world today, holiness is being despised

> *"For God hath not called us unto uncleanness, but unto holiness. He therefore that despiseth despiseth not man, but God, who hath also given unto us his Holy Spirit." 1Thessalonians. 4:7, 8*

The reason why it seems that holiness is impossible today is because it is not given its rightful position. Many people believe in holiness but in their personal life and ministry, wrong position is given to it.

A true Christian teaching and right positioning of things can help a believer to live holy every day of his life and except that, Christianity will continue to have problem in this aspect.

"That he would grant unto us, that we being delivered out of the hand of our enemies might serve him without fear, in holiness and righteousness before him, all the days of our life."

Luke. 1:74, 75

Anything you give priority to your life and ministry, takes over and rules others. If you give prosperity priority and in your ministry, it takes over holiness priority, it takes over salvation priority. Believers, leaders and ministers have to come back to re-order their priority and give holiness her rightful position otherwise things will continue to go the way they are going or even get worse.

The few churches that rightly place salvation and holiness should also give prosperity, breakthrough, deliverance and other doctrines things their right place, other-wise many people in their fellowship many get to heaven like Lazarus and others may curse God and die.

"And there was a certain beggar named Lazarus, which was laid at his gate, full of sores, And desiring to be fed with the crumbs which fell from the rich man's table: moreover the dogs came and licked his sores. And it came to pass, that the beggar died, and was carried by the angels into Abraham's bosom: the rich man also died, and was buried;" Luke 16:20-22,

"Then said his wife unto him, dost thou still retain thine integrity? Curse God, and die." Job 2:9.

Some holiness preachers today also despise wealth, prosperity and deliverance, while some prefer to stay in the middle road, on the fence in between two options.

"Two things have I required of thee; deny me them not before I die: Remove far from me vanity and lies: give me neither poverty nor riches; feed me with food convenient for me: Lest I be full, and

deny thee, and say, who the Lord is? Or lest I be
poor, and steal, and take the name of my God in
vain." Proverbs 30:7-9.

Without holiness, Christian life will be out of balance and life out of balance brings failure. A ministerial failure is one whose preaching is misplaced and emphasis is placed unduly on one or two misplaced subjects or doctrine.

When Christian experiences are rightly put in order with salvation and holiness given their rightful position, things will work out fine. If holiness is enthroned over all others, with salvation well placed as the pillar and foundational basic experience, the devil will bow.

Believers will not backslide or be carried away in times of prosperity, adversity, temptation etc when this Christian experiences are rightly placed. Our songs at all times should promote salvation first and holiness second, thereafter any other thing can follow as you desire.

What is holiness to start with? Holiness is the state of being free from sin internally and externally. Holiness is a state of having perfect love to God and man unreservedly. Holiness is the state of having all forms of carnality purged out of our life from inside to outside. Holiness is the state of total commitment to God and to be more mindful of heavenly things than earthly things. Holiness is living your life without spot or wrinkle. Holiness is a state of moral blamelessness before God. It is a state of life and conduct that promotes cleanness of heart and sober character. Holiness is God's way of giving a believer abundant life of joy, peace etc. It is not external conformity with religious duties without inner purity. Holiness is not the ability to pray long, fast long or dress very well as a Christian. Holiness is not the ability to preach very well with signs and wonders. Holiness is not frowning your face or looking haggard. Holiness is an experience that happens instantly. Believers don't grow into holiness until you have the initial experience. You can only grow into holiness to pursue to God's level after you must have been sanctified and made holy

"But as he which hath called you is holy, so be ye holy in all manner of conversation; Because it is

written, Be ye holy; for I am holy." 1Peter 1:15,
16.

It is a definite experience and it does not come gradually.

CHAPTER EIGHT

EXPERIENCING HOLINESS

One who experiences holiness will know it the same way he knew when he was saved. We should understand that God who wills for our holiness has also made adequate provision for it.

> *"Who gave himself for us, that he might redeem us from all iniquity, and purify unto himself a peculiar people, zealous of good works." Titus. 2:14.*

> *"Wherefore Jesus also, that he might sanctify the people with his own blood, suffered without the gate." Hebrew. 13:12.*

To experience holiness, you must know the importance of what you want and recognize the need in your life (Psalm. 51:7-10). Ask yourself some questions like, do I really need this experience at all cost? Am I easily irritated? Am I completely dead to sin and the world? Do I loose my peace easily? What are my intentions, thoughts and motives? Do I have the grace to bear reproaches and forbear misrepresentation? Do I fear God more than man? Am I jealous over other people's position? Am I always too conscious of my personality? If your answers are yes to these questions, then you need holiness. If you are quick tempered, habour unforgiveness and easily provoked you need to possess this experience.

To experience holiness, you need to take the following steps.

1. Get closer to God.

2. Be earnestly thirsty and pray for it. (Matthew. 5:6).

3. Leave all your sacrifices in the altar.

4. Whole heartedly consecrate your life to God holding back nothing (Psalm. 118:27).

5. Run away from all sorts of evil that will affect you (Job. 31:1).

6. Have a conscience void of offence towards God and men.

7. Be calm in your spirit man.

8. Be careful, prayerful and watchful.

9. Have faith in God as you pray.

10. Believe God that it is possible and that he is able to sanctify you.

Holiness experience is very easy because it is God's will and His promise. He derives joy when we are sanctified and made holy. Finally, in the office of God, many are specially called to emphasis on certain things like deliverance, faith, prosperity etc. But none is to be carried out at the expense of salvation and sanctification, because without the above two experiences, no one can enter heaven.

"Jesus answered and said unto him, Verily, verily, I say unto thee, except a man be born again, he cannot see the kingdom of God." John. 3:3.

"Follow peace with all men, and holiness, without which no man shall see the Lord:" Hebrew. 12:14

CHAPTER NINE

HOLINESS OR HELL? DECIDE NOW

The decision to go to heaven or enter hell fire is taken while we are in this planet earth. The roads to these two destinations are open to all that will pass through this life. All the preachers and prophets of God who had earlier lived, had always shown people of their generation the two ways. Men, as a free moral agents with the power of choice, are left with any of the options.

"Now therefore fear the Lord, and serve him in sincerity and in truth: and put away the gods which your fathers served on the other side of the flood, and in Egypt; and serve ye the Lord. And if it seem evil unto you to serve the Lord, choose you

this day whom ye will serve; whether the gods which your fathers served that were on the other side of the flood, or the gods of the Amorites, in whose land ye dwell: but as for me and my house, we will serve the Lord." Joshua. 24:14, 15

For those who choose heaven, holiness is compulsory because there is no alternative. Holiness is very important for all that want to spend eternity with God, though it is the most despised by people in the church today. A lot of people in the church have mocked, criticized and despised holiness and made a fool of all the people that preach it. However, God demands for holiness and commands it. Whatever God does, and each time he wants to make a move, holiness is always his demand.

"And ye shall be holy men unto me: neither shall ye eat any flesh that is torn of beasts in the field; ye shall cast it to the dogs." Exodus. 22:31

God's command and warning to his people of all generation is to avoid anything that can bring defilement. Whatever we want to do or we are already doing to God and for God should be done in the beauty of his holiness.

> *"Give unto the Lord the glory due unto his name: bring an offering, and come before him: worship the Lord in the beauty of holiness." 1Chronicles. 16:29*

The purpose of deliverance from anything, sickness, poverty, death etc is so that we can serve God without fear, in holiness and righteousness all the days of our life. God's deliverance and sanctification should be perfected and that is the will of God for every believer.

> *"That he would grant unto us, that we being delivered out of the hand of our enemies might serve him without fear, In holiness and*

righteousness before him, all the days of our life."

Luke. 1:74, 75

The wish of God for every believer is for us to live and overcome every careless moment, second, minute, hour, day, week, month, and year, all the days of our life.

"As obedient children, not fashioning yourselves according to the former lusts in your ignorance: But as he which hath called you is holy, so be ye holy in all manner of conversation; because it is written, Be ye holy; for I am holy." 1Pet.er 1:14-16

God's demand is for us to be holy as He, God is holy, and not as any other person is holy. No body is to be placed as a standard in our aspiration to be holy, God should be our standard. In every activity of believers on this earth, God demands holiness so as to partner with us because He is a holy God. Jesus Christ practiced holiness. At salvation, the Lord imparted His Holy Spirit unto us not an evil spirit. Our standard is the holy bible and heaven where we are going to is holy. Therefore, those who will get to heaven must be holy.

WHAT IS THE QUALIFICATION TO HEAVEN?

Many religious groups today talk about holiness and heaven as doctrine attached to their belief but they differ in the practice. Even among the so called children of God, the Christians, have disagreement on this matter. In the days of David, many of his admirers assured him of a place in heaven after death. People all over were praising him. The women of Israel composed a song for him. David was highly gifted in playing musical instrument. His harp and music brought healing to troubled souls. He was devoted to the service of God. He boldly faced Goliath and defeated him. The whole children of Israel including his enemies saw him as a hero. He was filled with noble deeds and great accomplishments. He was the choice of God to replace King Saul. David in his life time and ministry composed many great spirit inspired songs that moved people towards God even up till today. He loved the presence of God and esteemed God above earthly things.

"For a day in thy courts is better than a thousand. I had rather be a doorkeeper in the house of my God, than to dwell in the tents of wickedness. For the Lord God is a sun and shield: the Lord will give grace and glory: no good thing will he withhold from them that walk uprightly." Psalm. 84:10, 11

With all these great qualities, people around David must have praised him beyond normal. They must have on their own, assured him of a place in heaven. People must have compared him to others and concluded that of a truth he was over qualified for heaven. But David is not a man to be deceived or a man that allows people to praise him out of heaven.

David knew the things happening to him inside. Only God and David knew what his thoughts, imaginations were David understood himself more than all the people around him. He knew certain actions he wanted to take but because of his position as a leader he decided not to. He knew that most of the good things people say about him were wrong. He also knew that only God can tell him the truth. He had probably in some occasions known that people who were closer to him understood his weakness but out of fear, they failed to let him know his weakness. He knew that some people who were close to him had discovered some of his weakness but still they praised him and ignored and feared to confront him because of the fear of loosing his favour. He knew people were praising him even when he was supposed to be blamed. All the people around him praised him even when he committed evil.

One day, because David did not want to be deceived, he went to God in prayers to know the qualification to heaven. He knew that it was only God that could tell him the truth without fear. He wanted the truth and the true standard set by God to qualify a person of any level into heaven. He addressed and directed his question to God and immediately God answered.

"Lord, who shall abide in thy tabernacle? who shall dwell in thy holy hill?" Psalm. 15:1

People who feel that God's standard is so high, go to men, preachers who will tell them what they like to hear. They go to men, preachers who don't believe in holiness. Once you miss holiness on this earth you have forever missed heaven.

"And as it is appointed unto men once to die, but after this the judgment:" Hebrew. 9:27

Anyone who wants to make heaven should stop listening to preachers and deceivers who do not believe in holiness. People should depend on God and his words that cannot fail, not on human being who does not believe even in heaven.

"He that walketh uprightly, and worketh righteousness, and speaketh the truth in his heart. He that backbiteth not with his tongue, nor doeth evil to his neighbour, nor taketh up a reproach against his neighbour. In whose eyes a vile person is contemned; but he honoureth them that fear the Lord. He that sweareth to his own hurt, and

changeth not. He that putteth not out his money

to usury, nor taketh reward against the innocent.

He that doeth these things shall never be moved."

Psalm. 15:2-5.

God in answer to the questions of David plainly gave him the only true qualification to enter heaven. The holiness that takes one to heaven is the type that produces the truth right from the heart. When you talk about holy God, heaven, you must talk about holiness and holy people.

"Who shall ascend into the hill of the Lord? Or

who shall stand in his holy place?" Psalm. 24:3.

"Blessed are the pure in heart: for they shall see

God." Matthew. 5:8.

For anyone to get to heaven, he or she must have a pure heart and pure tongue. To see God at last you must be holy.

"Husbands, love your wives, even as Christ also loved the church, and gave himself for it; That he might sanctify and cleanse it with the washing of water by the word, That he might present it to himself a glorious church, not having spot, or wrinkle, or any such thing; but that it should be holy and without blemish." Ephesians. 5:25-27.

From the above reference, the qualification to heaven is sanctification, spotlessness without wrinkle, holiness without any blemish.

"Follow peace with all men, and holiness, without which no man shall see the Lord:" Heb. 12:14. "And the four beasts had each of them six wings about him; and they were full of eyes within: and they rest not day and night, saying, Holy, holy, holy, Lord God Almighty, which was, and is, and is to come." Rev.elation 4:8.

Our God is holy heaven is holy, and those who will be qualified to enter into heaven must be holy.

> *"And there shall in no wise enter into it any thing that defileth, either whatsoever worketh abomination, or maketh a lie: but they which are written in the Lamb's book of life." Revelation. 21:27.*

God will not permit anything or any person that has any form of defilement to enter into heaven. No abominable person or any manner of lie wills be permitted into heaven. Every sin must have been overcome to its root on this earth before anyone will be allowed to enter into heaven.

CHAPTER TEN

CLARIFICATIONS ON HOLINESS

Many preachers today have different beliefs about what holiness is. People have left the old path. Many are saying what they do not know. A lot of people base holiness on what pastor so and so has said or what their church believes. But in the days of Isaiah and other great prophets, they came out and said, thus said: the Lord" God. We have to go back to the old path to discover the true meaning of holiness.

"Because my people hath forgotten me, they have burned incense to vanity, and they have caused them to stumble in their ways from the ancient paths, to walk in paths, in a way not cast up;" Jeremiah. 18:15.

When people backslide, they teach false doctrine and try to modify the standard set up by God.

> *"Thus saith the Lord, Stand ye in the ways, and see, and ask for the old paths, where is the good way, and walk therein, and ye shall find rest for your souls. But they said, we will not walk therein." Jeremiah. 6:16.*

People are no more interested in going to God to discover the truth. No time to study the scriptures, yet they preach errors to deceive the mind of the simple. Because people can no more study the bible to discover the truth, they now chose the easy way which leads to destruction.

> *"Enter ye in at the strait gate: for wide is the gate, and broad is the way, that leadeth to destruction, and many there be which go in thereat: Because strait is the gate, and narrow is the way, which*

leadeth unto life, and few there be that find it."

Matthew.7:13, 14

Preachers who preach complete holiness as the only way to heaven are very few. The religious world on the other way are many. The gates of Jerusalem normally get closed at a particular time many years ago. The Israelites who come when the gates are closed normally pass through the small gate called nidle gate. But before they enter into the city with their horses, they will first offload all that the horses are caring and cross them through the nidle gate one by one. Anyone that cannot enter though the nidle gate stays outside the gate. But today in the church, preachers are no more talking about holiness. They are no more talking about condition to heaven. At salvation, anyone can come to God as he is but when he becomes a believers there is need for screening. At salvation, God's invitation is for all. At sanctification, before we qualify for heaven, there must be screening. We must drop both the inward and outward evil character and enter with the holy character. No one is allowed to enter into heaven with impure heart.

"And an highway shall be there, and a way, and it shall be called The way of holiness; the unclean shall not pass over it; but it shall be for those: the wayfaring men, though fools, shall not err therein. No lion shall be there, nor any ravenous beast shall go up thereon, it shall not be found there; but the redeemed shall walk there: And the ransomed of the Lord shall return, and come to Zion with songs and everlasting joy upon their heads: they shall obtain joy and gladness, and sorrow and sighing shall flee away." Isaih. 35:8-10.

The road that leads to heaven cannot permit any traveler without holiness. It is a way of holiness for holy people going to holy heaven to meet the holy God.

Nobody with any manner of uncleanness will be allowed to pass over it. Nobody with the character of beast shall be allowed to go up thereon. No one of such character shall be allowed or found on that road. The road is for the redeemed of the Lord who are ransomed. The road to heaven is different from the way to church. You may find your way to the church but if you are not holy, you will not find your way to heaven. You may manipulate your way to the office of your leader but if you are not holy, you will never find your way to the high way of holiness. You may manipulate your way into the position of the leadership in a church, but if you are not holy, you will not get to the high way of holiness. With your immoral life, you may still find your way to the office of your general overseer but if you fail to depart from your immorality, you cannot find your way to heaven. Holiness is the only way to heaven. You may be in the company of the most senior pastors in your church but without holiness, no man shall see the Lord. You may walk out from the prostitute house every Sunday morning into a church to pay your tithes gotten from your prostitution but if you don't repent and forsake your sin, you will never enter heaven without holiness. May be your pastor is afraid of telling you that those who are polygamous can never walk into this road unless they repent restitute and get sanctified. May be you may be a fraudster (419) and still every Sunday you walk into the church and at the end of the service you are the first person that sees your pastor for prayers. Listen to me, you can walk to any place, the most beautiful and great countries of the world but without holiness you can not walk to heaven.

You may be smoking and yet speaks in tongue. You may walk into any great man of God with defiled heart but no one is allowed to walk on the high way of holiness with any unclean heart.

"Awake, awake; put on thy strength, O Zion; put on thy beautiful garments, O Jerusalem, the holy city: for henceforth there shall no more come into thee the uncircumcised and the unclean. Shake thyself from the dust; arise, and sit down, O Jerusalem: loose thyself from the bands of thy neck, O captive daughter of Zion. Depart ye, depart ye, go ye out from thence, touch no unclean thing; go ye out of the midst of her; be ye clean, that bear the vessels of the Lord." Isaih. 52:1, 2, 11.

Depart here, means to depart from evil association. Do not touch another man's wife or daughter and all that are not married both in your office or school. Leave sin alone if you must be holy.

"Nevertheless the foundation of God standeth sure, having this seal, The Lord knoweth them that are his. And, Let every one that nameth the name of Christ depart from iniquity." Timothy. 2:19.

Believers who will be holy must leave sin alone and depart from iniquity.

Holiness is not just coming to church and belonging to a group in the church. It is not living above external sin. It is not working hard or walking very carefully or talking slowly in a low voice. It is not crying when you are talking to attract self pity. It is not saying it is well, God bless you or by shouting halleluiah, the Lord is good. It is not a special way of dressing or the way you appear in the church. It is not your outward comportment. It is not the ability to pray, preach and teach the word of God. It is not looking unhappy, not laughing or relating with people. It is not speaking in tongues or casting out devils.

Jesus clearly said that without holiness no one can get to heaven. That is the qualification. A preacher who taught that two plus two is equal to four will not mark you right if in an exam you said that two plus two is seven. But even if he will mark you right, Jesus is not a man that He can change. His qualification still remains the same. Holiness is not being legalistic. Holiness is not sleeping on the ground or not putting on good and clean clothes. It is not fasting or not eating good food. Holiness is not drinking garri or eating one type of food every day. It is not praying quietly or shouting when praying. It is not bowing down while harbouring evil in your heart. It is not keeping quiet when you should talk.

What then is the clarification of holiness? Holiness is possessing the very nature of God. It is being gentle as God and having the pure nature of God.

"Be ye therefore followers of God, as dear children;" Ephesians. 5:1.

Holiness is thinking and having the imagination of God

"But as he which hath called you is holy, so be ye holy in all manner of conversation; because it is written, Be ye holy; for I am holy." 1Peter. 1:15, 16.

"That ye may be the children of your Father which is in heaven: for he maketh his sun to rise on the evil and on the good, and sendeth rain on the just and on the unjust." Matthew. 5:45.

When you are holy, you will be able to relate with sinners and believers without committing sin. Holiness is the absent of sin both internally and externally

"That he would grant unto us, that we being delivered out of the hand of our enemies might serve him without fear, In holiness and righteousness before him, all the days of our life" Luke 1:74, 75.

Holiness is having absolute love of God.

"Jesus said unto him, Thou shalt love the Lord thy God with all thy heart, and with all thy soul, and with all thy mind." Matthew. 22:37.

Holiness is loving God to any level.

"Whom have I in heaven but thee? And there is none upon earth that I desire beside thee." Psalm. 73:25.

Holiness is walking with God with a perfect heart. Holiness is having no spot or wrinkle.

"Wherefore, beloved, seeing that ye look for such things, be diligent that ye may be found of him in peace, without spot, and blameless. 2 Peter. 3:14

CONSECRATION FOR HOLINESS

Anything someone gives out to be sanctified is worth it. Believers should not withhold anything that will hinder them from being sanctified and made holy. And the truth is that many believers have given priority to other things than sanctification. Holiness is very jealousy like every other Christian experience when they are neglected or despised. When money, position, power, material things, prosperity are emphasized or given priority after salvation, to attain to holiness experience will be very difficult unless you sacrifice that thing at the altar of God.

Holiness experience comes and goes when its position is taken by any other thing else. Praying to God to sanctify you when you know that you prefer prosperity, position or money more than holiness is very wrong. Prosperity, money, position and power are very good but giving them priority over holiness in your life or ministry is very wrong.

Emphasis may be given to the specific ministry you receive from the Lord like faith, deliverance, prosperity etc but they must not take the place of holiness experience in your life or ministry.

Once it is done, you may never attain to the level of holiness experience because true holiness can never accept the second best or accept to take a wrong positioning. As you pray, cry and probably fast to be sanctified, God will answer but it will not last, because holiness can never occupy wrong position.

Many believers must give up certain positions, humble themselves and rush to the altar of God and offer themselves to God afresh to receive true sanctification.

"I beseech you therefore, brethren, by the mercies of God, that ye present your bodies a living sacrifice, holy, acceptable unto God, which is your reasonable service. (Which he had promised afore by his prophets in the Holy Scriptures,)" Romans 12:1, 2

There are so many believers today who are occupying some high positions in the church. They are really born again, called by God but they are not sanctified. When they initially got born again, they pursued money at all cost and got it. They pursued power at all cost and got it. They pursued position and fought for it and got it. They pursued properties, ministry and fought for them at all cost to the expense of every other thing and got them.

Now, deep inside them, there is no peace, no rest. They have life to a certain measure but there is no abundant life. They have the love of God but their love is partial because they practice divide and rule. Their love is not perfect and fear gripes them every time. The shoot of sin rears its ugly head in their lives and the roots of sin reigns and rules in their lives. They are not destroyed and cannot just be destroyed at salvation. They need real sanctification to uproot the old man. Such believers are really praying for sanctification, they want to live a holy life but they insist on retaining what they have already which were wrongly acquired. They enjoy the presence of God at times but it comes and goes. They are free from sin but they are not completely free indeed because they still yield to some passions. They sin, repent and confess their sins and God forgives them but they are never free from sin indeed because the presence of the root of sin is still in charge. They are not free from inward sin.

They repent and confess sins all the time because occasionally, their hearts boil. They entertain worldly lusts, manifest revengeful spirits, manifest hot tempers, dress worldly with worldly adornment and compete with the world. They were worried over their low spiritual level and some of them need a change.

"For we know that the law is spiritual: but I am carnal, sold under sin. For that which I do I allow not: for what I would, that do I not; but what I hate, that do I. If then I do that which I would not, I consent unto the law that it is good. Now then it is no more I that do it, but sin that dwelleth in me. For I know that in me (that is, in my flesh,) dwelleth no good thing: for to will is present with me; but how to perform that which is good I find not. For the good that I would I do not: but the evil which I would not, that I do. Now if I do that I would not, it is no more I that do it,

but sin that dwelleth in me. I find then a law, that, when I would do good, evil is present with me. For I delight in the law of God after the inward man: But I see another law in my members, warring against the law of my mind, and bringing me into captivity to the law of sin which is in my members. O wretched man that I am! Who shall deliver me from the body of this death? I thank God through Jesus Christ our Lord. So then with the mind I myself serve the law of God; but with the flesh the law of sin. Romans. 7:14-25

Few got the change and experience the life of holiness and testified it. They paid the price and enjoyed full deliverance from the nature of sin;

"Though I might also have confidence in the flesh. If any other man thinketh that he hath whereof he might trust in the flesh, I more: Circumcised the eighth day, of the stock of Israel, of the tribe of

Benjamin, an Hebrew of the Hebrews; as touching the law, a Pharisee; Concerning zeal, persecuting the church; touching the righteousness which is in the law, blameless. But what things were gain to me, those I counted loss for Christ. Yea doubtless, and I count all things but loss for the excellency of the knowledge of Christ Jesus my Lord: for whom I have suffered the loss of all things, and do count them but dung, that I may win Christ, And be found in him, not having mine own righteousness, which is of the law, but that which is through the faith of Christ, the righteousness which is of God by faith: That I may know him, and the power of his resurrection, and the fellowship of his sufferings, being made conformable unto his death; Philippians. 3:4-10

Many believers still love their position more than the experience of sanctification thinking that God can be mocked or deceived. They keep to all that they have which have been wrongly gotten and positioned wrongly but they keep suffering from the dominion of sin. They have dominion over prosperity, they are delivereds from every sickness, poverty, death but they are not yet delivered from the dominion of sin.

"Because that which may be known of God is manifest in them; for God hath shewed it unto them. Professing themselves to be wise, they became fools," 26 "For this cause God gave them up unto vile affections: for even their women did change the natural use into that which is against nature. And even as they did not like to retain God in their knowledge, God gave them over to a reprobate mind, to do those things which are not convenient;" Romans. 1:19, 22 26 28

It is very unfortunate to say this hard truth. Many believers of every rank, some church founders, general overseers are living in immorality, adultery, unforgiving spirit, anger, revengeful spirit, worldliness, love of money, murder and abominations today. Yet, they still prosper materially, financially, and cast out demons. They still pray and miracles takes place and great deliverance are recorded in their ministries.

"Not every one that saith unto me, Lord, Lord, shall enter into the kingdom of heaven; but he that doeth the will of my Father which is in heaven. Many will say to me in that day, Lord, Lord, have we not prophesied in thy name? And in thy name have cast out devils? And in thy name done many wonderful works? And then will I profess unto them, I never knew you: depart from me, ye that work iniquity." Matthew. 7:21-23

If you despise holiness and give it a second class position in your life after salvation, you despise God and not man. If you want power at all cost even to the expense of your sanctification, you are likely going to get it but in the last day, you will regret it because God will look at you and say,

"I never knew you: depart from me, ye that work iniquity".

There is a great question in the bible that says:

> *"what shall it profit a man if he gains the whole world and lost his soul" "Though I speak with the tongues of men and of angels, and have not charity, I am become as sounding brass, or a tinkling cymbal. And though I have the gift of prophecy, and understand all mysteries, and all knowledge; and though I have all faith, so that I could remove mountains, and have not charity, I am nothing. And though I bestow all my goods to feed the poor, and though I give my body to be burned, and have not charity, it profiteth me nothing." 1Corinthians. 13:1-3*

For true holiness to come, you must pay the price by sacrificing the things or the experience you give priority to for holiness. You must give up certain things and come empty as you are and give yourself as an offering unto the

Lord. Prayer alone cannot do it, you need to sacrifice something. There must be a commitment on your side.

"Wherefore say unto them, Thus saith the Lord God; Ye eat with the blood, and lift up your eyes toward your idols, and shed blood: and shall ye possess the land? Ye stand upon your sword, ye work abomination, and ye defile every one his neighbour's wife: and shall ye possess the land? Say thou thus unto them, Thus saith the Lord God; As I live, surely they that are in the wastes shall fall by the sword, and him that is in the open field will I give to the beasts to be devoured, and they that be in the forts and in the caves shall die of the pestilence. For I will lay the land most desolate, and the pomp of her strength shall cease; and the mountains of Israel shall be desolate, that none shall pass through. Then shall they know that I am the Lord, when I have laid the land most desolate because of all their abominations which they have committed." Ezek. 33:25-29

Many unsatisfied believers have built empires around themselves. They are not ready to compromise their ill gotten wealth, political acquired positions, hypocritical fake holiness. But the truth is that no body can mock God or deceive Him. Their empires shall be most desolate and the pomp of their strength shall cease.

For the humble who will listen to the voice of the Holy Spirit, obey, and commit to perfection of their hearts, the Lord says that he will establish their hearts to become unblameable in holiness before God from now to the end at the coming of our Lord Jesus Christ. It is God that sanctifieth and your part is to obey and commit your life to heart purity and you will see it happen.

"To the end he may stablish your hearts unblameable in holiness before God, even our Father, at the coming of our Lord Jesus Christ with all his saints." 1 Thessalonians 3:13.

CHAPTER ELEVEN

DELIVERANCE FROM FAKE HOLINESS

From all that we have studied so far, you can see that the whole world is full of fake and Christianity is not exempted.

"Having a form of godliness, but denying the power thereof: from such turn away." 2 Timothy.3:5

Many believers have been diverted to fake holiness which are not acceptable to God and cannot take anyone to heaven. Of everything that God does, Satan will always bring his imitation to enslave the souls of men. But thanks be to God who has given us the true scriptural standard and the right holiness to heaven.

TRUE BIBLICAL REQUIREMENT TO HEAVEN

The second time I traveled out of my country for missionary work, I was at the international air port with my luggage. I had my flight ticket as an evidence of my right to join the aircraft to take me outside the shores of my country. I was on the line and the immigration officers were busy searching and screening every passenger. Unknown to me, I forgot my passport booklet at my ministries international officer. I totally forgot everything about my international passport. Everybody was being checked and those certified by the immigration department officials were allowed to join the air craft and their passports were stamped. On each of the passport the custom or immigration stamp will be stamped on the passport e.g. 03A or some other numbers written; SEEN ON DEPARTURE and date will be written, then the immigration officer on duty will sign. Immediately, you will face another set of screening and searching by different officers from another nation probably of different color, language and laws. If you are cleared, your passport will again be stamped SEEN ON ARRIVAL, date and the officer will sign and on the same passport the visa will be there and duration of your stay in that nation will be indicated.

That evening of my travel for missionary work was a busy day for me as I was running up and down. When it reached my turn, I presented my flight ticket but behold my passport was not included. For that reason, I was pushed aside and asked to go for my passport, though I had other documents, paid fully for my flight but I was disqualified and refused entry into that country not even into the flight that I have fully paid for. I had the right to fly, enter into another country but I was not fit, why? I had no passport. Even in the local flights, land, sea and other means of traveling, you have a condition to meet, before you can be taken to your destination. Before you leave your country to another, you need a passport to get there. What type of passport does the bible talk about as requirement to another country? You may have a passport that has no visa inside it. With that type of passport, you cannot get to another country. If your passport is tempered with and notification made on it by the immigration officer of any country, you may not get into that country. If a particular page is removed especially where your photograph is and other vital information, nobody will allow you to enter into any country with that type of strange passport. If the page of the passport is stained, you may need to do something about it. We are talking about physical things. And as it is in the physical so it is in the spiritual and even more serious.

It is very unfortunate to say that millions of believers have lost their passport completely without knowing it. You may have other documents but without passport, you will not move. Many millions of Christians have a stained passport etc. They still have other documents, they still operate with the gifts of the Spirit but their passports are stained. They sing very well, pray fervently, conduct powerful programmes and signs and wonders takes place. They occupy enviable positions, preach powerfully, call powerful prayers points but they have no heavenly passport.

Unfortunately, because of these other documents they fail to notice that their passports are stolen, marked bad and written VISA denied.

The problem is that what many millions of believers are holding firm today are not heavenly passports. Millions of Christians all over the world are struggling to have ministry without passport; promotion and position without passport; gifts of the Holy Ghost without passport, fame, money, prosperity and power, without passport. You may manipulate the earthly immigration and enter into any country without passport. You may bribe your way into any place, get any thing you want with your long leg without qualification, but no one, no matter how manipulative or influential can dribble the heavenly immigration. Christians who have the heavenly passport, declare plainly that they seek for a better country. They are not mindful of anything that will stand to stain or rob them of their heavenly passport. They are not mindful of this present place. They are not planning to remain forever in this earth. Their desire is not here but in the heavenly place, a better country. They talk about heaven, where God is, His son, the Holy Spirit and the heavenly angels. They despise anything that will deny them entry into that country but they don't despite holiness.

> *"For they that say such things declare plainly that they seek a country. And truly, if they had been mindful of that country from whence they came*

out, they might have had opportunity to have returned. But now they desire a better country, that is, an heavenly: wherefore God is not ashamed to be called their God: for he hath prepared for them a city." Hebrew 11:14-16

No matter who you are, you are preparing for another country. True believers who are sanctified and made holy are going to a better country.

"For here have we no continuing city, but we seek one to come." Hebrew. 13:14

This present country will soon expire and that is why we are seeking for a better country which will never expire

"Nevertheless we, according to his promise, look for new heavens and a new earth, wherein dwelleth righteousness. Wherefore, beloved, seeing that ye look for such things, be diligent that

ye may be found of him in peace, without spot, and blameless." 2Peter. 3:13-14

We are preparing for heaven and heaven cannot admit anything or person that is not holy. The heaven we are preparing for is full of God's righteousness, peace without spot or blemish.

"And I saw a new heaven and a new earth: for the first heaven and the first earth were passed away; and there was no more sea." Revelations. 21:7-8

"He that overcometh shall inherit all things; and I will be his God, and he shall be my son. But the fearful, and unbelieving, and the abominable, and murderers, and whoremongers, and sorcerers, and idolaters, and all liars, shall have their part in the lake which burneth with fire and brimstone: which is the second death." Revelation. 21:1, 7, 8

The first heaven and earth will not continue forever. The overcomer shall inherit all things even what they had to loose to gain this holiness. There are many things to overcome in this world because heaven is not bread and butter. The overcomers who will get to heaven must overcome evil, false prophets, the world, sin and Satan in this present world.

"And there shall be no more curse: but the throne of God and of the Lamb shall be in it; and his servants shall serve him:" "And there shall be no night there; and they need no candle, neither light of the sun; for the Lord God giveth them light: and they shall reign for ever and ever." "Blessed are they that do his commandments that they may have right to the tree of life, and may enter in through the gates into the city. For without are dogs, and sorcerers, and whoremongers, and murderers, and idolaters, and whosoever loveth and maketh a lie." Revelations. 22:3, 5, 14, 15.

We are preparing for a better country where there is no more curse. We are preparing for a better country where there shall be no night or the need of candle. Where light is not needed nor sun allowed to operate. The inhabitants of that better country shall be granted free access to the tree of life. That is why we must do all things do-able, possible to keep our passport and visa updated and unstained by the powers of this world. But the first question is, are you born again? If your answer is yes, when were you born again? How did it happen and where did it take place?

"Jesus answered and said unto him, Verily, verily, I say unto thee, except a man be born again, he cannot see the kingdom of God. Jesus answered, Verily, verily, I say unto thee, except a man be born of water and of the Spirit, he cannot enter into the kingdom of God." "Marvel not that I said unto thee, ye must be born again." John. 3:3, 5, 7

These questions are very important because we were all born in sin. Sin has disqualified every one of us and the need to be born again is hanging on every one on earth. We need to reconcile with God and be born again, transformed and renewed. Every one need to acknowledge his or her sins, repent, confess and ask God for cleansing of all sin.

Jesus confronted Nicodemus with this word born again.

> *"Know ye not that the unrighteous shall not inherit the kingdom of God? Be not deceived: neither fornicators, nor idolaters, nor adulterers, nor effeminate, nor abusers of themselves with mankind, Nor thieves, nor covetous, nor drunkards, nor revilers, nor extortioners, shall inherit the kingdom of God." 1Corinthians. 6:9,10.*

> *"Not every one that saith unto me, Lord, Lord, shall enter into the kingdom of heaven; but he that doeth the will of my Father which is in heaven. Many will say to me in that day, Lord, Lord, have we not prophesied in thy name? And in thy name have cast out devils? And in thy name done many wonderful works? And then will*

I profess unto them, I never knew you: depart from me, ye that work iniquity." Matthew. 7:21-23

Not everyone that goes to church is born again. Not all the members of the church who sing, pray, preach, prophecy, dream, perform signs and wonders are born again. Not all the miracle workers, people who heal the sick or do other mighty works are born again. It is possible to do all these things and yet not being born again.

To perform wonderful works with the name of Christ without living above sin is not holiness. It is fake to count yourself holy just because you perform signs and wonders without bearing the fruit of the Spirit. God demands perfection of the heart as a true holiness, not miracles without fruits.

"Blessed are the pure in heart: for they shall see God." Matthew. 5:8

From the above bible reference, we are taking a step further. This is beyond being born again. There are many things the devil can bring into your heart to dirty your heart and keep you defiled. You may be a leader in the church but if you have impure heart, you are not holy. If you still manifest evil thoughts, bitterness and yet you claim to be holy simply because you can cast out demons, your holiness is fake. Living a sinful life can allow you to have a passport but such passports are defiled and they cannot take you to a better country. Immorality and lust can defile your passport. If Jesus comes at the time you are entertaining evil thoughts or any sin, you have no passport that can take you to a better country. Millions of believers have lost the passport they used to have before. At their initial conversion, they use to love the bible, they even prayed for their enemies, loved the children of God, went out for evangelism but today, they have lost their passports. What they have now is fake Christianity, fake holiness.

At the beginning of their Christian race they were filled with the fruits of the Spirit.

"But the fruit of the Spirit is love, joy, peace, longsuffering, gentleness, goodness, faith, Meekness, temperance: against such there is no law." Galatians. 5:22, 23.

But now, they are filled with grudges, criticism, malice, anger, immoral thoughts and yet, they process to be holy still. They steal church money and yet they profess to be holy. That holiness is fake. You need real deliverance. There are many people in the church today who are eating the forbidden fruit, yet they claim to be holy. We have so many Cains in the church today in leadership position. They are killing their Abel while claiming to be the most senior, the foundation members of the church. They claim to be born again and have made holy. They said that they are sanctified but their sanctification is fake, it needs deliverance. We have in the church today wives of Lot who are already converted to a pillars of salt, yet they are claiming to be holy. Many are like the daughter of Lot who plan and commit abomination and incest in the church, yet they profess to be holy. We have so many Labans today in many churches, cheating Jacob and exploiting the gifts of God in his life, yet they profess to be holy. There are many graceless ladies like the wife of Potipher, who are troubling Joseph in the office, house and every where, yet they claim to be born again, sanctified and baptized in the Holy Ghost. Many today are like the sons of Aaron, who still sacrifice, preach in the temple of God but of a truth, they are offering strange fire. They still claim to be born again and made holy but their holiness is not the biblical holiness that can take one to heaven.

In the church today, even among ministers, we have a lot of ministers who complain, lust after flesh and commit immorality and yet they sing holy songs in the pulpits. Right inside the churches today among the leadership, we have great people like Dathan, Korah and Abiriam who always gather to fight God's constituted authority and yet they convince everybody that they are holy. That may be holiness but it is not the biblical holiness that can take anyone to holy heaven.

"Now Korah, the son of Izhar, the son of Kohath,

the son of Levi, and Dathan and Abiram, the sons

of Eliab, and On, the son of Peleth, sons of Reuben, took men: And they rose up before Moses, with certain of the children of Israel, two hundred and fifty princes of the assembly, famous in the congregation, men of renown: And they gathered themselves together against Moses and against Aaron, and said unto them, Ye take too much upon you, seeing all the congregation are holy, every one of them, and the Lord is among them: wherefore then lift ye up yourselves above the congregation of the Lord?" Numbers. 16:1-3

There are many leaders, pastors, members who are in the church for the sake of making money. They are in the battle field only to make money. They steal church money, mismanage church funds and tell lies to cover up, yet they preach sound message as if they were holy. They rob Peter to pay Paul. They put their unconverted royalists in great leadership positions and yet they claim to be holy. That may be holiness but we are talking about biblical holiness.

"Now Jericho was straitly shut up because of the children of Israel: none went out, and none came in." Joshua 7:1

"But the children of Israel committed a trespass in the accursed thing: for Achan, the son of Carmi, the son of Zabdi, the son of Zerah, of the tribe of Judah, took of the accursed thing: and the anger of the Lord was kindled against the children of Israel." Joshua. 6:1 7:1, 11-15

"Israel hath sinned, and they have also transgressed my covenant which I commanded them: for they have even taken of the accursed thing, and have also stolen, and dissembled also, and they have put it even among their own stuff. Therefore the children of Israel could not stand before their enemies, but turned their backs before their enemies, because they were accursed: neither will I be with you any more, except ye destroy the accursed from among you. Up, sanctify the people, and say, sanctify yourselves against to morrow: for thus saith the Lord God of Israel,

There is an accursed thing in the midst of thee, O Israel: thou canst not stand before thine enemies, until ye take away the accursed thing from among you. In the morning therefore ye shall be brought according to your tribes: and it shall be, that the tribe which the Lord taketh shall come according to the families thereof; and the family which the Lord shall take shall come by households; and the household which the Lord shall take shall come man by man. And it shall be, that he that is taken with the accursed thing shall be burnt with fire, he and all that he hath: because he hath transgressed the covenant of the Lord, and because he hath wrought folly in Israel." Joshua 7:11-15

Saul favoured some people in the time of his rule. He gave his royalists leadership positions and drove away a man who was anointed. He tried his best to kill David who saved the children of Israel from Goliath. To the people from the tribe of Saul, he is holy man of God but God rejected him. His holiness was not accepted. Even when he backslid and sought for a woman with a familiar spirit, he was still seen as holy by the people of Benjamin. He became wrath and eyed to kill David, took away David's wife but because he is a foundation member, a tribes man, he was still holy in the sight of the people from Benjamin. Even after eating at the house of an enemy of God, a witch, some of his people still regarded him and went out with him to fight wars. To them, he was a holy man of God because he gave them inheritance, a branch of a church to pastor and an assignment in a foreign land. That is not a biblical holiness even though people see it as holiness, it is a tribal holiness without God. The type of holiness that takes people to heaven was seen and described by Isaiah

"And an highway shall be there, and a way, and it shall be called the way of holiness; the unclean shall not pass over it; but it shall be for those: the wayfaring men, though fools, shall not err therein. No lion shall be there, nor any ravenous beast shall go up thereon, it shall not be found there; but the redeemed shall walk there: And the ransomed of the Lord shall return, and come to

Zion with songs and everlasting joy upon their heads: they shall obtain joy and gladness, and sorrow and sighing shall flee away." Isaiah. Is. 35:8-10

These kinds of holiness need deliverance because they are fake holiness. The holiness that takes away the right people from office and put in the wrong ones and the holiness that puts hands at the Holy Ark is not the right holiness. Any holiness that disobeys God's commandment is not a biblical holiness. The holiness that helps God where he is not needed is not a biblical holiness

"And when they came to Nachon's threshingfloor, Uzzah put forth his hand to the ark of God, and took hold of it; for the oxen shook it. And the anger of the Lord was kindled against Uzzah; and God smote him there for his error; and there he died by the ark of God. And David was displeased, because the Lord had made a breach upon Uzzah: and he called the name of the place

Perez-uzzah to this day. And David was afraid of the Lord that day, and said, how shall the ark of the Lord come to me? So David would not remove the ark of the Lord unto him into the city of David: but David carried it aside into the house of Obed-edom the Gittite. And the ark of the Lord continued in the house of Obed-edom the Gittite three months: and the Lord blessed Obed-edom, and all his household." 2Samuel. 6:6-11

Now, ask yourself what kind of holiness are you practicing? Is it the holiness that plan adultery and execute it? Is it the holiness that defiles other men's wives and invites their husband for a dinner with their wives? Is it a holiness that gives contracts to other men's wives to defile them and invite their husbands to eat and drink? Is it a holiness that gives accommodation to immoral women while you plan to kill their husbands? Is it a holiness that commits abortion to protect your evil and cover your crime? Is it a holiness that pays school fees to the children of your staff so that you can have immoral relationship with their wives? What kind of holiness are you practicing?

> *"And it came to pass in an evening tide, that David arose from off his bed, and walked upon the roof of the king's house: and from the roof he saw a woman washing herself; and the woman was very beautiful to look upon. And David sent messengers, and took her; and she came in unto him, and he lay with her; for she was purified from her uncleanness: and she returned unto her house. And the woman conceived, and sent and told David, and said, I am with child. And the shooters shot from off the wall upon thy servants; and some of the king's servants be dead, and thy servant Uriah the Hittite is dead also. And when the mourning was past, David sent and fetched her to his house, and she became his wife, and bare him a son. But the thing that David had done displeased the Lord."* 2Samuel. 11:2, 4-5, 24, 27 2

If this is the kind of holiness you are practicing, your holiness need an emergency new testament deliverance.

All over the word today in the body of Christ, costmetic holiness is taking over. There is jewelry competition and worldliness which is becoming the order of the day. It is difficult to differentiate between the believers and unbelievers today. Everybody is claiming to be holy even with all the worldly dressing competition of chains, gold and bangles imported from the Egypt. Christianity is becoming more worldly than the world. Before, the world had their way of dressing, adornment but today, it is freely seen in the churches. The churches today are demonstrating worldly fashion that exposes nakedness.

"And when thou art spoiled, what wilt thou do? Though thou clothest thyself with crimson, though thou deckest thee with ornaments of gold, though thou rentest thy face with painting, in vain shalt thou make thyself fair; thy lovers will despise thee, they will seek thy life. For I have heard a voice as

of a woman in travail, and the anguish as of her
that bringeth forth her first child, the voice of the
daughter of Zion, that bewaileth herself, that
spreadeth her hands, saying, Woe is me now! For
my soul is wearied because of murderers."
Jeremiah. 4:30-31

With all these nude dressing, people still say that they are holy.

"Rise up, ye women that are at ease; hear my
voice, ye careless daughters; give ear unto my
speech. Many days and years shall ye be troubled,
ye careless women: for the vintage shall fail, the
gathering shall not come. Tremble, ye women that
are at ease; be troubled, ye careless ones: strip
you, and make you bare, and gird sackcloth upon
your loins. They shall lament for the teats, for the
pleasant fields, for the fruitful vine. Upon the land
of my people shall come up thorns and briers; yea,
upon all the houses of joy in the joyous city:

Because the palaces shall be forsaken; the multitude of the city shall be left; the forts and towers shall be for dens for ever, a joy of wild asses, a pasture of flocks;" Isaih. 32:9-14.

The holiness that need deliverance is the one that resemble the world.

"For though thou wash thee with nitre, and take thee much sope, yet thine iniquity is marked before me, saith the Lord God." 34 "Also in thy skirts is found the blood of the souls of the poor innocents: I have not found it by secret search, but upon all these." Jeremiah. 2:22, 34.

"How shall I pardon thee for this? Thy children have forsaken me, and sworn by them that are no gods: when I had fed them to the full, they then committed adultery, and assembled themselves by troops in the harlots' houses. They were as fed

horses in the morning: every one neighed after his neighbour's wife." Jeremiah. 5:7, 8

There are other people in the church I want to bring to our attention. These groups also practice fake holiness. They are found among the rich people. They are among the executives. They sponsor church projects, give accommodation to some highly placed pastors. They don't bother much about prayers because they trust in the prayers of the pastors, so they are prayer collectors. Any time they need prayer even from big general overseers and other ministers they get it without much stress. They help the poor, assist many people who need their assistance but most of them are not born again. The few that are born again are not sanctified. They believe that the prayers of the pastors can help them and secure them a place in heaven. They are self righteous people. They come to church when they have chance. Some of them have special seat in the church with their names written on those seats. They love believers, feed them, cloth them and at times buy cars for the pastors but this type of holiness is fake. They still with all the above good deeds, need bible holiness. The reason is because if they die with this kind of holiness, they will go to hell fire.

"There was a certain rich man, which was clothed in purple and fine linen, and fared sumptuously every day: And there was a certain beggar named Lazarus, which was laid at his gate, full of sores, And desiring to be fed with the crumbs which fell from the rich man's table: moreover the dogs came and licked his sores. And it came to pass, that the beggar died, and was carried by the angels into Abraham's bosom: the rich man also died, and was buried; And in hell he lift up his eyes, being in torments, and seeth Abraham afar off, and Lazarus in his bosom. And he cried and said, Father Abraham, have mercy on me, and send Lazarus that he may dip the tip of his finger in water, and cool my tongue; for I am tormented in this flame. But Abraham said, Son, remember that thou in thy lifetime receivedst thy good things, and likewise Lazarus evil things: but now

he is comforted, and thou art tormented. And beside all this, between us and you there is a great gulf fixed: so that they which would pass from hence to you cannot; neither can they pass to us that would come from thence. Then he said, I pray thee therefore, father, that thou wouldest send him to my father's house: For I have five brethren; that he may testify unto them, lest they also come into this place of torment. Abraham saith unto him, they have Moses and the prophets; let them hear them. And he said, nay, father Abraham: but if one went unto them from the dead, they will repent. And he said unto him, if they hear not Moses and the prophets, neither will they be persuaded, though one rose from the dead." Luk.e 16:19-31

Many humble brethren who were genuinely converted, sanctified and filled in the Holy Ghost are no more with the heavenly passport. Their holiness is no more pure. What they now operate with is counterfeit. They now select people they love and hate others. I will not listen to these ones preaching, he is not qualified to be my leader. To them, they no more tolerate nonsense. They now consider age, education, tribe and do unprofitable comparison. Some say such things as: "If not that I am a woman, he is not qualified to talk before me". "I am sorry to say this, he is not my class". It is just that we are in the same church. If he is working in my office, he is not up to my secaretary. Humility has departed from the dictionary of many believers who once were humble and an example to others. The desire to live a holy life has departed from them. At the initial stage, when they first got born again, their words were healing for the sick, comforting to the discouraged and their suggestions encouraged and were timely. But now, the reverse is the case. They now have many enemies and they are no more following peace with all men. They are ready to disagree with everybody and as a result, everyone is afraid of them because they are ready to fight, tell lies, gang up, write false petitions.

Even upon all these, they still claim to be born again. This is not biblical born again or holiness. Everything is now fake and deliverance is needed urgently. *"Follow peace with all men, and holiness, without which no man shall see the Lord:"*

Heb. 12:14

CHAPTER TWELVE

WHAT IS BIBLICAL HOLINESS?

True biblical holiness is the holiness that affect both inside and outside.

> *"Who shall ascend into the hill of the Lord? Or who shall stand in his holy place? He that hath clean hands, and a pure heart; who hath not lifted up his soul unto vanity, nor sworn deceitfully."*
> *Psalm. 24:3, 4*

True biblical holiness touches the hands and the heart. It affects the soul condition and manifests outside

"Ye are witnesses, and God also, how holily and justly and unblameably we behaved ourselves among you that believe:" 1Thessalonians. 2:10.

True biblical holiness destroys every form of unrighteousness, deceit and brings salvation inside the soul and causes sin to perish. When such things take place, the people around will notice it and testify of it.

Many years ago, women who truly received this touch were known because their characters changed with their outward appearance. It affected their mode of dressing. Women who claim to be born again but still dress like men have not really experienced true biblical holiness. They dress like men but they refuse to do hard work like men. Their dressing, Jeweries are their God.

"And when Jehu was come to Jezreel, Jezebel heard of it; and she painted her face, and tired her head, and looked out at a window." 2Kings. 9:30.

True biblical holiness manifests in the following:

1. Inward and outward holiness:

They are known by hunger and thirst after righteousness right from inside. No matter how righteous they are, they still desire more. They want to be like God, not like any other person. They pursue inner and outward purity and they can pay any price to get it.

> *"Blessed are the meek: for they shall inherit the earth." 8 "Blessed are the pure in heart: for they shall see God." Matthew. 5:5, 8*

The fruit of the tree of righteousness in them does not bring corrupt fruit but good fruits.

> *"For a good tree bringeth not forth corrupt fruit; neither doth a corrupt tree bring forth good fruit. For every tree is known by his own fruit. For of thorns men do not gather figs, nor of a bramble*

bush gather they grapes." Luke. 6:43, 44. (1Peter. 1:15, 16, Matthew. 5:48, Titus. 2:14).

2. Inner victory and freedom:

True biblical holiness brings sanctification and cleansing and makes the heart blameless without spot or wrinkle. It keeps a person free from offence till the day of Christ and filled with the fruit of righteousness. It gives abundant life and sets one perfectly free indeed.

"That he might sanctify and cleanse it with the washing of water by the word, That he might present it to himself a glorious church, not having spot, or wrinkle, or any such thing; but that it should be holy and without blemish." Ephesians. 5:26, 27.

True biblical holiness keeps the soul alive and energizes believers for zealous work of God (Philippians. 1:9-11, John. 10:10 8:36).

3. Oneness and unity:

True holiness brings believers in unity and love with one another together with Christ.

> "Neither pray I for these alone, but for them also which shall believe on me through their word; That they all may be one; as thou, Father, art in me, and I in thee, that they also may be one in us: that the world may believe that thou hast sent me. And the glory which thou gavest me I have given them; that they may be one, even as we are one: I in them, and thou in me, that they may be made perfect in one; and that the world may know that thou hast sent me, and hast loved them, as thou hast loved me." John. 17:20-23.

It binds believers together and makes them to live in peace and to love to one another. When you see two sisters or brothers who cannot live together in love, peace and unity in a place, the problem is because they do not have biblical holiness.

"Endeavouring to keep the unity of the Spirit in the bond of peace." Ephesians. 4:3.

Another evidence of true biblical holiness is, they are mindful of one thing and they strive together for the faith of the gospel. They have unity of doctrine, one goal and common vision for eternity

"Only let your conversation be as it becometh the gospel of Christ: that whether I come and see you, or else be absent, I may hear of your affairs, that ye stand fast in one spirit, with one mind striving together for the faith of the gospel;" Philippians. 1:27.

They speak one language, they are united in the spirit and in the unity of language. They are glad whenever and wherever they meet together. They have joy in fellowshipping together.

> *"Behold, how good and how pleasant it is for brethren to dwell together in unity! It is like the precious ointment upon the head, that ran down upon the beard, even Aaron's beard: that went down to the skirts of his garments; As the dew of Hermon, and as the dew that descended upon the mountains of Zion: for there the Lord commanded the blessing, even life for evermore."*
> *Psalm. 133:1-3*

4. Right motives:

They have the same mind with Christ and they live or die only for Christ. They are servants to Christ and they live to please Christ than pleasing man.

> *"For do I now persuade men, or God? Or do I seek to please men? For if I yet pleased men, I should not be the servant of Christ." Galatians. 1:10.*

Their honour comes from God and they do not seek or fight for human honour (Jn. 5:41, Phil. 2:51, 21).

5. Perfect love:

They love God with all their heart with perfect love. They love one another as Christ loves them, not as the world loves.

> *"This is my commandment, that ye love one another, as I have loved you. Greater love hath no man than this that a man lay down his life for his friends." John. 15:12, 13.*

They also keep God's commandment and lay their lives to save fellow believers who are in trouble.

> *"Hereby perceive we the love of God, because he laid down his life for us: and we ought to lay down our lives for the brethren." 1John. 3:16*

Their love is perfect, bold without fear. True biblical love is rooted and grounded in love and they are linked up together with other believers. True biblical holiness believers does not act disorderly; they are not forward, ill minded, impolite or rude to people no matter their level. Holiness of life is the most important Christian experience that can take a believer to heaven. The price is great; no human under heaven can pay for it. But I have a good news for you, some one has paid for it. It is free off charge. The only thing a believer need now is to believe that with God all things are possible.

"Wherefore Jesus also, that he might sanctify the people with his own blood, suffered without the gate." Hebrews. 13:12

For believers to be sanctified and made holy, Christ took up the position of the believer and suffered on his behalf. Among all that Christ died for on the cross of Calvary, our sanctification experience is included. He shed his blood, suffered without the gate for our sanctification experience. There is no salvation and sanctification outside the blood of

Jesus Christ. No believer can reject the blood of Jesus Christ and receive sanctification experience. The blood of Jesus is our sanctifier. His perfect, spotless, sinless blood went outside the gate and was shed to sanctify us. What believers need now to be truly sanctified and made holy is to believe God and thirst for the experience. To be hungry to be like Jesus.

"Blessed are they which do hunger and thirst after righteousness: for they shall be filled." Matthew. 5:6.

The next step to take is to pray in faith because God does not do anything except in prayer.

"And I say unto you, Ask, and it shall be given you; seek, and ye shall find; knock, and it shall be opened unto you. For every one that asketh receiveth; and he that seeketh findeth; and to him that knocketh it shall be opened." Luk.e 11:9-10

As you pray and by God's grace you get sanctified, do everything to remain in the experience. Do not allow anything to rob you of this great experience. Watch and pray all the time and as much as possible be at peace with every one. Do all within your reach to abide in Christ and beware of any little or big sin. Do not ever compromise your faith in any little way no matter what, lay all to the altar.

"And Jesus arose, and followed him, and so did his disciples. And, behold, a woman, which was diseased with an issue of blood twelve years, came behind him, and touched the hem of his garment: For she said within herself, If I may but touch his garment, I shall be whole." Matthew. 6:19-21

THANK YOU!

I wanted to take this opportunity to appreciate you for supporting my ministry and writing career by purchasing my book. I'm a full-time author and every copy of my book bought helps tremendously in supporting my family and that I continue to have the energy and motivation to write. My family and I are very grateful and we don't take your support lightly.

You've done so much for me already but I need you to do me one more favor if you can spare a moment of your time. Please I need you to go to the link below and give me your honest review. This is important because it helps me sell more books.

CLICK HERE TO LEAVE A REVIEW

Please note that I read and appreciate every feedback. Also note that you do not have to have finished reading the book before you can leave a review. You can just share with me what you think of what you've read so far. You can always come back later if you wish and update your review.

Once again, here is the link:

CLICK HERE TO LEAVE A REVIEW

Thank you so much as you spare this precious moment of your time and may God bless you and meet you at every point of your need.

Please send me an email on prayermadu@yahoo.com if you encounter any difficulty in leaving your review.

Other Books By Prayer Madueke

1. 100 Days Prayers to Wake Up Your Lazarus

2. 15 Deliverance Steps to Everlasting Life

3. 21/40 Nights of Decrees and Your Enemies Will Surrender

4. 35 Deliverance Steps to Everlasting Rest

5. 35 Special Dangerous Decrees

6. 40 Prayer Giants

7. Alone with God

8. Americans, May I Have Your Attention Please

9. Avoid Academic Defeats

10. Because You Are Living Abroad

11. Biafra of My Dream

12. Breaking Evil Yokes

13. Call to Renew Covenant

14. Command the Morning, Day and Night

15. Community Liberation and Solemn Assembly

16. Comprehensive Deliverance

17. Confront and Conquer Your Enemy

18. Contemporary Politicians' Prayers for Nation Building

126. Youths, May I Have Your Attention Please?

Free Book Gift

Just to say Thank You for getting my book: Power to Pray once and Receive Answers, I'll like to give you these books for free:

<u>Click here</u> to download these books now

If you're reading this from the paperback version, email me at <u>prayermadu@yahoo.com</u>.

Your testimonies will abound. <u>Click here</u> to see my other books. They have produced many testimonies and I want your testimony to be one too.

An Invitation To Become A Ministry Partner

In response to several calls from readers of my books on how to partner with this ministry, we are grateful to provide our ministry's bank details.

Be assured that our continued prayers for you will be answered according to God's word. And as you remain faithful by sowing seeds of faith, God will never forget your labors of love in Christ.

Send your Seed to:

In Nigeria & Africa

Bank Name: Access Bank

Account Name: Prayer Emancipation Missions

Account Number: 0692638220

In the United States & the rest of the World

Bank Name: Bank of America

Account Name: Roseline C Madueke

Account Number: 483079070578

Routing Number (RTN): 021000322

Visit the donation page on my website to donate online: www.madueke.com/donate.

Printed in Great Britain
by Amazon